# Pieces of Eight

*The Rites, Roles, and Styles of the Dean*

*By Eight Who Have Been There*

**James R. Appleton**

**Channing M. Briggs**

**James J. Rhatigan**

*Clarence N. Anderson*
*Consulting Editor*

*Published by*
*NASPA Institute of Research and Development*
*National Association of Student Personnel Administrators*
*P.O. Box 751, Portland, Oregon, 97207*

## PRODUCTION AND DESIGN NOTES

The text of this book was set in Palatino, 11 on 13. Headings are in 18-point Palatino, capitals and lower case, with subordinate heads in 12 point. Feature quotations within the Oxford rules are in 11-point Korinna.

Cover design: Ben Cziller. Typographic design: C.N. Anderson. Composition: Alphabet Type Shop, Portland, Oregon. Printing and binding: Malloy Lithographing, Ann Arbor, Michigan.

## RIGHTS

Library of Congress Catalog No. 78-52999.

ISBN No. 0-931654-00-9.

# Dedication

The authors do not claim omniscience, nor even a superior brand of sagacity, in student affairs. We have simply toiled strenuously, conscientiously—and long enough—to qualify us as experienced, if not expert, in our field.

In this book we hunch our collective shoulders together, on which the newcomer or young administrator may stand and reach higher than have the authors. Certainly it behooves the aspiring dean, now moving through the labyrinth of social, cultural, administrative, and political passageways that could lead to large student affairs duties, to spend time with this book. The "eight who have been there" would be pleased to know that, by standing on our shoulders, others may have a higher and surer reach in their service and in their careers than they otherwise may have had. To those who follow, then, this book in part is dedicated.

As concerned as the authors are about competent succession, even closer to our hearts as the chapters emerged were the families, friends, and colleagues who attended—not always with quiet patience—the gestation of this book. Over 150 years of service to various campuses is represented in the careers reflected in its pages. Too much of that time came out of private hours—hours that should have been spent with those close.

Mark Smith put it poignantly when he asked, "Dean, you have 676 Saturdays until your children are 14. How many do you owe them?" The twinges that come with that thought apply as well to personal time with all of those close—family, friends, associates. For the hours that should have been spent with them but instead were spent on this book—or on other missions that our profession dictates—we ask of them understanding, and to them, also, we dedicate this book.

# Acknowledgements

In addition to the eight contributor-authors, much is owed to a number of other collaborators.

The NASPA Central Office staff became veteran transcribers, as some 800 pages of material attested. Jan McDonald, Jane McCaig, Robin Thomas, and Barbara Portwood bore much of the original transcribing responsibility.

Similarly, Paul Moore, Kelly, and Sylvia Pope reinforced Jim Appleton's double role as contributor-author and co-editor. Clarence Anderson, University Editor at USC, was an active participant throughout: consulting editor, graphic designer, production coordinator. Paul Bloland provided important recommendations.

Jack Boland became the transcriber of Earle Clifford's documentary. Nancy Smith, Gloria Blackburn, Doris Peters, and the John Lowes hosted the interviewer generously.

To all of these colleagues, NASPA and its eight presidents are grateful.

# Pieces of Eight

*The Rites, Roles and Styles of the Dean*
*By Eight Who Have Been There*

Introduction . . . . . . . . . . . . . . . . . . . . . . . . . . . . . . . . . . . . . . . .1

A Corrective Look Back . . . . . . . . . . . . . . . . . . . . . . . . . . . . . .9

On Deaning and Learning . . . . . . . . . . . . . . . . . . . . . . . . . .43

Authority: Given, Earned, Presumed, and Lost . . . . . . .55

Organization and Relationships . . . . . . . . . . . . . . . . . . . . .65

Some Plan, Some Play Catch Up . . . . . . . . . . . . . . . . . . .83

There Was Almost No Chapter on Discipline . . . . . . . .99

Decision, Decisions, Decisions . . . . . . . . . . . . . . . . . . . .105

Staff Training and Development . . . . . . . . . . . . . . . . . . .113

Kisses of Death . . . . . . . . . . . . . . . . . . . . . . . . . . . . . . . . . .129

Styles of the Dean . . . . . . . . . . . . . . . . . . . . . . . . . . . . . . . .139

Our Future Is Showing . . . . . . . . . . . . . . . . . . . . . . . . . . .157

Memo to the President . . . . . . . . . . . . . . . . . . . . . . . . . . .165


Appendix—The Odyssey . . . . . . . . . . . . . . . . . . . . . . . . . .185

# Introduction

THE INSTITUTE FOR RESEARCH AND DEVELOPMENT of the National Association of Student Personnel Administrators (NIRAD) came into being during the NASPA presidency of John L. Blackburn. He believed that over time NIRAD could serve as a living endowment in service to student affairs administrators throughout the nation.

Potential projects for the new Institute were discussed in 1975. It was agreed in principle that the Board should consider issues that were beyond the annual NASPA operating budget. The first project, obviously, had to face the reality of a small budget, dollars provided by donors who agreed to provide initial support for the Institute. The endeavor was expected to encourage gifts, which it did in some measure, to demonstrate the viability of the Institute as a generator of worthwhile enterprises leading to advancement of student affairs work.

> "The book might be for the aspiring and the uninspired, the NASPA member, the library . . . even the unemployed. Better yet, we should write it for ourselves."

After reviewing alternatives at Airlie, Virginia, and later in Denver, the Institute board agreed to pursue as its first project the publication of a book emphasizing the role and style of the student affairs dean. It was agreed that the book should draw on the experiences and the common, garden variety savvy of successful administrators, rather than upon the jargon and data-encumbered forms that identify traditional research and scholarship. Although the former might draw a questioning look from the research-oriented, reality and relevancy were on its side.

The notion of the "successful" administrator presented an obvious problem. Many successful deans have never been elected to an office, enjoy little if any visibility apart from their own or surrounding campuses, and may not even have contributed notably to the literature. It was eventually acknowledged that to attempt to locate and then to interview a representative number of "successful" deans would be impractical. Instead, the past eight presidents of the National Association of Student Personnel Administrators were selected. These eight had been voted by their peers to lead a professional organization recognized for its contribution to the practice, literature, and general advancement of the field; have a collective tenure of more than a century; and each has made a demonstrable contribution to the profession. Why just eight presidents? No sufficient justification probably exists, but it was generally felt that the period of the 70s provided enough breadth, depth, sheer variety, and force of example to give the book both historical perspective and practical immediacy.

The focus of the potential publication was to be upon administrative style, its underlying values and competencies. The context, of course, was to be higher education; the application, to student affairs deaning. The material was to be generated by experienced administrators critical of themselves and each other, not by critics, professors, or anyone else who might have a view of the dean. The vehicle was to be a carefully structured interview, gathered, to the extent possible, on the campuses of the eight administrators.

Although the more detached view of an external critic was thus sacrificed it was felt that such critical treatment is already available from a number of sources. Nowhere, however, is there a resource compiled from the impromptu but incursive remarks of deans willing to let their thoughts take form with the coffee-stained, shirt-sleeve candor of a typical dean under normal late-morning siege, with a lunch appointment waiting at the Faculty Club.

The eight deans met together once, in Washington, D.C., in October 1976, prior to a meeting of the Executive Committee. In that day-long session, important priorities in the working lives of the eight NASPA presidents and the basic structure of the opus were put in focus. Earlier, NASPA Executive Director Channing Briggs and Jim Appleton had developed a questionnaire covering a range of topics. That questionnaire was used to direct a full day of interviewing by Briggs, with each of the eight contributor-authors. The resulting material covered more than 800 pages of transcription, all of which had to be categorized into chapters, formatted, edited, reviewed, recycled, and re-edited. In some instances, the editors unabashedly provided some connective tissue to tie together gaps in the emerging literary organism.

The long task of writing and editing could be looked upon as a celebration of the efficacy of spare-time and overtime effort in tackling an awesome assignment. As could be expected, the project enjoyed enthusiastic participation and response in its first stages but mixed feelings as it passed through successive cycles. Practical men and angels would have avoided the project like Hank Aaron avoided the low, outside ones, but "the NASPA Eight" moved into it as though the pitcher had hung a high curve. The logistics were as far-flung as they were formidable; the time schedule, intense as it was unremitting.

Because the deans showed interest in the "why" as well as the "how" of their work, the book quickly took on the aspect of a compendium of practical knowledge and counsel rather than of an administrative cookbook. Concept, principle, and value received more attention than ready-made recipes for handling the daily grist or for guiding individual performance. As "performers," in fact, the eight NASPA presidents have quite different individual styles. Yet, Briggs, whose efforts were indispensable to the project, observed that underneath those styles lay significant and unmistakable commonalities.

Perhaps these commonalities help explain the ascendancy of these NASPA presidents. In summarizing their characteristics, Briggs noted that the eight deans are versatile and varied in addressing diverse issues but remarkably comparable in the following:

- Though their work rhythms are quite individualistic, they all convey a high level of energy.

- They are clearly initiators and innovators more than responders and imitators.

- They have learned to cope effectively with daily pressures, uncertainties, and ambiguities in their total responsibility as well as in their detailed duties.

- Each exemplifies the capacity to bring complex tasks to a successful finale.

- Each employs a fairly compact set of administrative principles in making decisions.

- Each enjoys a reputation for relating easily with students, staff, faculty, and colleagues.

- Each is inclined to review and analyze information thoroughly and to apply it to maximum value.

- Each places the highest possible premium upon competence and integrity—in themselves no less than in their staffs.

Many administrators can perform well when conditions are favorable. The best test of competence, however, occurs under profoundly unfavorable conditions. All eight were administrators during the late 60s, when working environments were far from ordinary. They confronted anger, tension, pettiness, fear, and ugly violence. Some of these manifestations occurred on the campus; some were directed toward the campus; but whether imported or domestic, the wine of those years was often bitter and the aftermath, acrid. Minimal guidelines were available: One's own skills and values were the primary resource. These deans survived the period with their reputations not only intact but enhanced, and their subsequent advancement in the field was an irrefutable measure of the increased esteem which their competence under fire earned them.

It was clear from the interviews that one sustaining influence undergirding them is an affirmation of life itself. This affirmation takes different forms, but it is clear in the work of each, as it surely is in the lives and work of many of their colleagues across the nation.

In the end, of course, administrators are known by the decisions they make. These decisions include great and small issues, involving people holding widely different values, in circumstances that are typically not fully known or understood. The automatic expectation is that these decisions will be correct without much homage to that elusive entity known as "doing the right thing." What are the moral and value positions that sustain one in making substantive decisions? How does one balance ideals against pragmatic needs and realities? How does one act in the face of human differences in strident contention? When must one prevail? Compromise? Retreat? What are the human costs—in morale, time, and energy—that must be paid as one proceeds through long years in the field? What sustains one dean and cripples another? What kinds of decisions are fatal to effective performance? How does one act sensibly when nonsense reigns? What are the constraints one must tolerate, ambiguities one must wrestle with, failures one must acknowledge? There are no ready-made answers to such questions, but they are certainly not abstractions. Clearly they are at the heart of the work of the dean.

This book underscores the concept of style, identifies challenges to it, and suggests that administration is as much art as science; it lives and moves and has its being in a moral arena. A chapter is devoted specifically to the dean's style, but even the chapters dealing with our professional history, with the sources of our authority, and with such administrative tasks as planning, administrative relationships, decision-making, and staff training and development belie the notion that the successful student affairs dean is a faceless deputy.

---

**There is not one administrative style. You achieve that style which is successful for you only by beginning with yourself and continuing to be yourself.—Clifford**

---

It should be noted that we have chosen "dean" as a generic term for the chief student affairs officer. Position titles are now changing, but in an historical sense, the term "dean of students" has clear meaning (Tripp, 1970; Moore, 1977).

Two years have passed since the idea of the book was introduced. Slowly, chapters have evolved from ruminations and responses. Interviews became tapes that became transcriptions that became shared and edited drafts. The original objective—to publish a book describing experience in administation as recounted by eight NASPA past presidents—has provided the underlying thrust, direction, and motivation. No stipend has been offered to tease a single phrase from any of them. Any net receipts from this effort will go to NIRAD, as John Blackburn envisioned.

Appleton and Briggs met together several times to cajole, reenforce, press, and criticize each other's efforts. They bear final editing responsibility for the effort, except the chapters on student affairs history by Rhatigan and "Kisses of Death" by Mark Smith, which appear essentially as written but with certain respectful (and respected) editing suggestions. The pace and flow of the Rhatigan and Smith chapters are unique, yet they stand out more because of the importance of the material presented than because of their literary flavor. Jim Rhatigan added substantially to the development of several chapters. Tom Dutton produced the original drafts of the chapter on planning and "On Deaning and Learning." Earle Clifford had the first go at the chapter on discipline. Included as an appendix is a detailed report of the travels and ruminations of Briggs—"The Odyssey."

If the book has at least partially succeeded in meeting its aims, it may become a prototype for further discourse and documentation among administrators on topics of common experience and concern. The authors invite comment and questions that may be supplementary, critical, or reenforcing: If sufficient and substantial, they may be the basis for a sequel. The art of administration in student affairs thus may become better known and better practiced.

Reading into this presentation an intent to preach or to proclaim with certainty would denigrate its purpose. As ambitious in scope and effort as the project became, the questions posed and the approaches documented still represent the thoughts of only a few persons in student personnel administration. The book only begins to explore available options. It simply addresses some of the common variety of preoccupations and concerns in the field. If it generates continuing interest and refines some

---

**All teaching is presumptuous, and I see this book as a teaching document.—Smith**

---

understandings of the complexity of student affairs administration, it will have more than fulfilled its promise, and perhaps the searching reader will have discovered a gold doubloon or two in this cache of *Pieces of Eight*.

## References

Moore, Paul L. *An Analysis of the Position of Dean of Students in Selected Institutions of Higher Education*. Unpublished Ph.D. dissertation, University of Southern California, 1977, p. 1.

Tripp, Philip A. Organization for Student Personnel Administration. *Handbook of College and University Administration: Academic*, Asa S. Knowles, Editor.

### The Past Eight Presidents of NASPA
(and most recent campus assignments)

Mark W. Smith, *Union College*
Earle W. Clifford, *Fairleigh Dickinson University*
Chester E. Peters, *Kansas State University*
Thomas B. Dutton, *University of California, Davis*
John L. Blackburn, *University of Denver*
James R. Appleton, *University of Southern California*
James J. Rhatigan, *Wichita State University*
Alice R. Manicur, *Frostburg State College*

### The Executive Director of NASPA
Channing M. Briggs

# A Corrective Look Back

FEW ADMINISTRATORS SEE THE RELEVANCE or importance of historical forces and issues to the present status of student affairs administration. This is a grievous miscalculation. History provides perspective and without an understanding of the role our predecessors played, the circumstances in which they worked, and the contributions they may have made to higher education in the United States, we have a truncated knowledge of our profession in particular and of campus development in general. In our field, the present is a dominant preoccupation. The price of this preoccupation is the diminution not only of our predecessors but also of ourselves.

With only a handful of people having an understanding of our history, it is not surprising to find a paucity of articles on the history of student personnel work. Of those who have commented on historical issues, few have been practicing administrators. This has resulted in a serious void; those who could provide a unique perspective have been unwilling or unable to do so. Perhaps they have been simply indifferent, failing to appreciate the value of historical writing to our field.

Some excellent documents that exist are seldom used. Some documentation has been lost, and of course it will never be recovered. But it is the history never recorded that might have been the most significant, involving the daily work of men and women who were too busy to consider writing, or who failed to leave ample records. History, as one writer put it, "is what evidence obliges us to believe," and our "evidence" has been insufficiently developed. *We must understand that, in substantial ways, professional identity is rooted in the past.* We cannot afford to continue a legacy of indifference.

Obviously, this chapter can do little justice to the history of our field. It may be useful, however, to review some issues that have contributed to the reputation accorded us by some writers (Penney, 1969; Brown, 1972; O'Banion and Thurston, 1972; Birenbaum, 1974) and to suggest that these views are rooted as much in stereotype as they are in scholarship. It is also hoped that as a result of this effort  other persons in our field with an interest in history will find their appetites whetted, and that additional work in this area will receive attention.

A corrective look backward may seem unduly defensive. To those who feel good about their work, it may even seem irrelevant. Vermilye (1973) has aptly observed, "If we defined ourselves by our deeds and how well we perform them, we would need no other definitions." It is the view of this writer, however, that we cannot escape history, as enriching or as damaging as it might be. Because an understanding of our past is necessary, it deserves our thoughtful, continuing attention. Whether we like what we find or not, the understanding gained from historical examination should help us to move ahead with greater confidence and perspective.

This chapter finds its way into a book dealing with the role and style of administrators because present roles and styles are a function of history. Throughout the observations offered by the eight administrators, history is at work, whether they know it or not. Our work today is firmly tied to the past, in the most direct possible sense; this is quietly, often unrecognizably, but surely true.

## Beginnings

Our work is largely a phenomenon of American higher education in the twentieth century, though its halting beginning is in evidence in the last quarter of the nineteenth century. Other writers have pointed to antecedents dating to the universities of the Middle Ages (Cowley, 1940) and to Athenian education (Bathurst, 1938).

The phenomenal growth and resilience of student personnel work are sources of constant amazement and its development vexing to many. Arguments abound as to whether it is a profession; some of its own practitioners show a lack of understanding about it; its future is frequently seen as tenuous; some prescient group or prophet is nearly always working at the task of reorganizing, reevaluating, reshaping, or renaming it. Some writers have suggested that the field came into existence because the president needed help in regulating student behavior. Clearly, a larger understanding is needed. Several factors influenced the development of this new field of work. The weighting these factors deserve, their interrelationships, and the way in which their individual impact varied from campus to campus are imprecisely understood.

Factors contributing to the origin of our profession would include: (1) the development of land-grant institutions and the rise of public colleges and universities; (2) increasing enrollments, and the accompanying increase in the heterogeneity of student populations; (3) social, political, and intellectual ferment in the nation; (4) the rise of coeducation, and the increase in numbers of women entering institutions; (5) the introduction of the elective system in higher education; (6) an emphasis on vocationalism over the traditional liberal arts, (or at least in growing competition with the liberal arts); (7) the impact of science and the scientific method; (8) the emerging signs of fundamental struggle between empiricism and humanism; (9) the apparent correlation between intellectualism and impersonalism on the part of faculty, notably those educated in German institutions; (10) expanding industrialization and urbanization, and the closing of the American "frontier"; (11) the view of higher education as a social status phenomenon, with less student commitment to "academic" subjects; (12) the establishment of a true "University" system; (13) the impact of liberal immigration laws in the United States; and (14) the changing roles of students in higher education. There were undoubtedly any number of other factors, but certainly all of those above are related to the changes that occurred, though one is not sure of the precise interplay.

For an understanding of the dramatic features of these changes, one must return to an earlier setting. The early American college was heavily value-oriented, with the president serving as the chief moral font. As Frederick Rudolph (1976) has observed, "moral purpose, values, and the reality of heaven," were dominant characteristics of those institutions and their prime administrators. College embraced the totality of the student but emphasized his spiritual needs. There were few public institutions, and the central religious emphasis did not erode until secular institutions gained a permanent foothold.

Nevertheless, it would be difficult to exaggerate the importance of public education. Because its value centers were not based in religion, its mission had to be developed differently. Some of the early public institutions were established to serve pragmatic needs (agriculture, technological subjects, home economics, etc.). The establishment of John Hopkins as the first legitimate American "university" had a dramatic and opposite effect. Institutions followed pell-mell in search of scholars interested in research;

a growing number went to Germany for their training, returning to the United States with that model of education in mind. They showed little interest in student life outside the classroom. As the number of elective courses grew, so did the fragmentation of higher education, and the resulting fractionalization of learning still exists today in most institutions.

During this period the moral force of the president was greatly diminished. His efforts were diverted to the problems of finance, capital construction, faculty recruitment, the establishment of new programs, and the politics of growth stemming from legislative bodies and lay boards. Problems of accommodating increasing numbers of students, many of whom were not well prepared for higher education, were demanding. Rudolph notes that the senior course in moral philosophy, often taught by the president of the old-time college, was its "most effective and its most transparent repository of values. . . . Once that course died, as in time it did, there would really be no way to prevent the formation of the National Association of Student Personnel Administrators" (Rudolph, 1976).

Contending philosophies were vigorously present during the period 1870-1920, and students were no more immune to them than was the larger population. The impact of these several philosophies upon education, and through education to the student affairs field, needs more careful examination. (Three examples are considered later in this chapter.) One thing is clear: A rapidly growing and heterogeneous population of students entered higher education needing substantive assistance in other than curricular matters at approximately the time much of higher education was jettisoning that responsibility. The early efforts to restore the concern and effort to help students were principal conditions leading to the birth and early growth of the field of student personnel administration. No one knew for sure what needed to be accomplished, or how, but only that needs were there. We began by serving needs that had been pushed to the periphery, and some would argue that the field has remained there ever since. Our existence was predicated upon being out of the mainstream; how to become (or whether to become) a part of the mainstream is our continuing dilemma, complete with contradiction, contumely, and irony. Whether this is the glory or the burden of the field is the prevailing subject of concern and discussion among those in the profession today—in random rap sessions at professional meetings. The concerns of the early deans of men and deans of women were not always incidental to higher education, but *only incidental to that period.* Before that, much of what these deans worried about had been central issues in higher education. The early deans were humanists in a venture increasingly dominated by empiricists. It probably is helpful to consider that if faculty at the turn of the century had viewed what we did as important, we probably would not exist in the organizational form found today. If, as has been suggested, we are a constant reminder to faculty of their failure to cope with the lives of students, we must then realize also that we are a source of unconscious resentment. This is a legacy we are capable of overcoming, if it indeed is true.

## The Dean and The Personnel Worker

While factors contributing to the emergence of the field may have been similar, they surfaced in different ways in different places. It is likely that few administrators understand that our work emerged from three separate sources: the dean of women, the dean of men, and the personnel worker. Their vestiges are still apparent in the existence of three major national organizations (NAWDAC, NASPA, and ACPA). Anyone doubting the influence of history should be advised of the several efforts to merge these three organizations. The inability to accomplish any merger can be traced to various conditions, but a dominant reason surely is the function of history.

There is some disagreement as to who the first dean might have been, and while this is not especially critical, this writer relies on the work of W.H. Cowley, who believes that the dean of deans was LeBarron Russell Briggs of Harvard, who assumed his position in 1890. Blackburn (1969) reports "dean of women" appointments as early as 1890 (Swarthmore) and 1892 (University of Chicago). Thomas Arkle Clark (Illinois) claimed to be the first administrator to carry the title "dean of men", beginning in 1909, though he assumed the responsibilities earlier.

It is difficult to understand why the deans of men and deans of women have fared so poorly in the way they are remembered. A review of the *Proceedings* of the early meetings of deans of men and deans of women reveals a great majority of persons having high ideals, warmth, optimism, and genuineness. They appear to have enjoyed the respect of and to have shown affection, compassion, and concern for students. They evidenced strong qualities of leadership. Most of them were deeply religious; it is interesting to observe that most came from backgrounds in the liberal arts;

our kinship with the liberal arts is a facet of our history that warrants more careful examination and articulation.

These men and women moved without the benefit of prior history, professional preparation, substantial financial support, clearly outlined duties, adequate communication across campuses, an agreed-upon sense of direction, or tools of any kind save their own values, skills, and leadership qualities. Nevertheless, they laid a foundation upon which a field of work could later be built. This was reflected in a growing professionalization, that developed with grudging but genuine recognition from other campus segments. This may not be a cheerful observation for those currently interested in "reconceptualizing" the field, but it is wholly supportable.

The early deans' positions emerged as they worked. As this writer has written elsewhere, the field developed from the campus up, not from the theory down (Rhatigan, 1975). Dean Stanley Coulter of Purdue observed: "When the Board of Trustees elected me Dean of Men I wrote them very respectfully and asked them to give me the duties of the Dean of Men. They wrote back that they did not know what they were but when I found out to let them know" (Secretarial Notes, 1928). Thomas Arkle Clark noted: "I had no specific duties, no specific authority, no precedents either to guide me or to handicap me. It was an untried sea upon which I was about to set sail. *My only chart was that the action of the Board of Trustees said I was to interest myself in the individual student"*(Secretarial Notes, 1924). Both of these early deans referred to trustees, causing one to wonder what role these Boards played in our history. Were trustees acknowledging requests from presidents, or was their role more active than that?

Definitions of the position of dean of men began to take shape as the deans examined their roles in the period roughly from 1910-1930. A typical definition was "that officer in the administration who undertakes to assist the men students (to) achieve the utmost of which they are individually capable, through personal effort in their behalf, and through mobilizing in their behalf all the forces within the University which can be made to serve this end" (Secretarial Notes, 1932). President Cloyd Heck Marvin of George Washington University observed, "The Dean of Men is most free to interpret his position in terms of modern University life because he is handling problems dealing with the adaptation of student life to the constantly changing social surroundings. . . . You are dealing in men, helping the student to get hold of life, to find the right environment in which he can develop himself to his fullest capacity" (Secretarial Notes, 1929).

The deans of men often commented about their basic roles but the illustrations above are typical of their views. It seems appropriate to suggest that their notion of "service" was quite different from that attributed to them by later writers (Brown, 1972; Crookston, 1972). Far from the analogy of "service station," the early deans' statements seem to stem in part from a religious orientation. It is also interesting to observe the frequency of their references to the "development of students," which some writers today see as unique to our own time. The early deans simply did not differentiate between "service" and "development," and one could take the view that the latter follows from the former. This is a matter of definition, but it is clear to this writer that the early deans of men and women (1) saw "service" as a much more fundamental phenomenon than have later writers, and also (2) that one aspect of the phenomenon was rooted in religion.

The issues facing the early deans of women overlapped those of their male counterparts, but had some understandably unique features. Many educators were unenthusiastic about the increasing enrollment of women students, feeling that they were physically and emotionally ill-equipped to cope with the rigors of higher education. As early as the mid-1800's we note the liberal Horace Mann, serving as president at coeducational Antioch College some years earlier, commenting on women's enrollment to the Regents of the University of Michigan, who were considering coeducation: "The advantages of a joint education are great. The dangers of it are terrible" (Holmes, 1939). He argued that either the moral dangers facing women would have to be dealt with or he would prefer that "young women of that age" not have the advantages of an education. Deans of women were expected to deal with these issues. The deans undoubtedly privately despaired of their situation, yet they took advantage of the opportunity to participate.

Most of the early deans of women were nonconformists. They were a first-of-a-kind in institutions that were first-of-a-kind (coeducational). The frustrations they encountered were enormous, a product of working in an alien environment dominated by men. It seems clear that they were treated with respect in a personal sense, but their ambitions for young women were not always respected. They were particularly irritated about the expectations of student discipline thrust upon them. Many male counterparts saw this as the central role of deans of women, whose annoyance over this attitude is apparent in the literature.

The precarious position of the deans of women affected their language, which was circumspect in every respect, and their behavior, which was more formal than that of the deans of men. But their purpose was clear: to enlarge the possibilities and influence the potential of the young women they served in every possible way.

In spite of a clear recognition of their disadvantaged status, these women tended to think and write in broad terms. In the first text of its kind, Mathews wrote: "The major opportunities (of the dean of women) are . . . educational, involving the varying roles of vocational preparation appropriate to higher education" (Mathews, 1915). Urging that the proper role for a dean of women was to be as a specialist in women's education, Mathews believed the position to have a primary and unique responsibility for an entire generation of young women. This sense of destiny did much to overcome the dean of womens' continual frustration, a function of the slow progress apparent to them. Mathews noted that any woman considering being a dean must be prepared to "run a wide gamut of joy and sorrow." This admonition seems appropriate even now.

Like their male counterparts, the position of dean of women varied greatly from campus to campus. In an early history of the position, Holmes (1939) observed that the position was not standardized and probably should not be. Holmes outlined many of the obstacles, opportunities, and quality programs found in her study of various campuses. For those who might be guilty of seeing these women as gray-haired ladies looking after routine chores, Holmes reports that sixty per cent had faculty rank and taught regularly. One would hypothesize that the early deans saw the recognition not only as earned, but essential to their reputations as deans. Fley (1963) has observed of these women that a remarkable breadth of interest, keen insight, and scholarship were evident from the beginning.

One is now left to inquire as to why only a stilted caricature remains as the legacy of these deans of women. Except for their own professional *Journal*, little attention has been paid to these remarkable women, except as "snooping battle-axes," as Fley puts it.

We have largely forgotten their essential courage in the face of formidable circumstances; their dedication in attempting to open new fields of study for women; their persistence even in failure; the stereotype they fought to overcome; the ethical standards evidenced in their work; the example they set for all who have followed. We have diminished them when they should stand as role models, rather a matter of ignorance than of malice, but the result is very nearly the same. In searching through a number of examples that might capture the views of these women, this writer selected a sentence by Kathryn Sisson Phillips, the first president of the National Association of Women Deans (NAWD), written shortly before her death: "Life can be good, but we must make it so, and we all have so much to give to each other along the way" (Cook, 1976). Romanticized pap? Probably the cynic will see it that way; but from any viewpoint, we have come a long way from the environment that spawned such feelings toward the role of women deans.

The third group comprising the field was the "personnel" worker. It should be pointed out, however, that no early dean of men or dean of women ever referred to the word "personnel."

In 1911, Walter Dill Scott, a psychologist at Northwestern University, published the first book known to apply principles of psychology to employees in industry. As World War I approached, Scott was asked to offer assistance to the U.S. Army to develop a classification system for the Army. In 1917, a Committee on Classification of Personnel was formed that, in retrospect, included a who's who of the emerging field of psychology, measurement, and educational psychology. Among them were E.K. Strong, Jr., E.L. Thorndike, W.V. Bingham, John B. Watson, Louis M. Terman, Robert M. Yerkes, and J.K. Angell.

When Scott accepted the presidency of Northwestern in 1919, he did so with the understanding that he could develop a personnel program for the institution. In a meeting with the Northwestern Board of Trustees, Scott described his concept of personnel work:

> It is my belief that the emphasis should be on the individuality of the student and his present needs and interests. The student should be looked upon as more than a candidate for a degree, he is an individuality that must be developed and must be trained for a life of service. . . . Inadequate attention has been given to the fundamental problem of personnel. The great problem in our nation today is the problem of people . . . (Blackburn, 1969).

The focus Scott chose was to guide students intelligently into the proper field of work, and vocational guidance was to be performed by the personnel administrator. Both the number of personnel workers and the variety of services they offered multiplied rapidly, but the emphasis on vocational guidance became such a dominant theme that, in time, for many, the terms "guidance" and "student personnel" were seen as nearly synonymous. One difficulty was apparent. The work Scott envisioned for the field entailed efforts already under way, having been organized by deans of men and deans of women. *On some campuses they coalesced immediately, but on others the groups worried about each other, and instances of hostility resulted.*

A number of events coincided with the work of Scott, involving the scholars engaged in the activities of the Army classification system. A discussion of this issue would require an historical outline of the study of psychology in the United States. This discussion is available elsewhere (Murphy, 1949; Boring, 1950), but the impact of these influences on the field of student personnel must be acknowledged.

The status of psychology in the United States was altered by John B. Watson. The introspective psychology which Wundt had formulated proved frustrating because it was found lacking in objectivity. Predictability was difficult and replication was nearly impossible. Lowe (1969) reports that disillusionment with introspection led to behaviorism, the application of the objective methods of animal psychologists to human beings. Watson wrote that "psychology as the behaviorist views it is a purely experimental branch of natural science" (Lowe quoting Watson, 1914). This opened a field of study that has been flourishing ever since. It is clear that the field of student personnel owes a debt to behaviorism, but as is characteristic of much of our dilemma, the weighting of that debt could be enhanced by historical analysis applied to our present status.

A second element in this time frame included a group of people interested in measurement. While Cattell has been credited with instituting the first American testing and data collection (at Columbia University), the work of Alfred Binet was of major influence. His tests were translated and produced in several versions, the most important of which was the Stanford-Binet, first produced by Lewis Terman in 1916. Thorndike and Strong, among others, turned their creative attention to the educational implications of psychological testing. The enthusiasm generated from developments in measurement was pronounced, but the field has had an uneven history. A reading of any issue of the *Personnel and Guidance Journal* today reveals the student personnel fascination with measurement, at a time when its tenets are under heavy attack elsewhere.

A third element in an understanding of the "personnel movement" concerns the social philosophy and hard work of Frank Parsons. Brewer (1942) summarized Parsons' work in thorough fashion, so it may be sufficient here merely to note that perhaps more than any one other individual, Parsons was responsibile for bringing to public consciousness the concept of "vocational guidance." His response to the cruelties of industrialism was timely and thoughtful. While his interests were directed toward public school youths, higher education embraced the guidance concept, and in 1911 Harvard offered a short course on the subject. John Brewer was appointed as a full-time faculty member at Harvard in 1916, to teach courses in vocational guidance. The use of the analytical tools previously noted were ready-made for those attempting to embellish Parsons' ideas.

A final "personnel" element emerged from the field of mental health. "It came to be recognized that mental health really depended on the way people got along with each other on the college campus. Increasingly, it was seen that it was closely tied up with the morale of the college, with the presence or absence of conflicts in the environment or within the personality" (Brubacher and Rudy, 1968). The general American public seemed ready for the development, as Clifford Beers' *A Mind That Found Itself*, published in 1909, was already well known. Mental health came to be seen as more than an absence of illness, involving preventive devices that should certainly be employed on the campus.

The work of John Dewey has a place of its own but the voluminous nature of that work cannot be approached here except to alert the reader. The issues of educational sociology and educational philosophy which Dewey (and his followers) brought to the schools were clearly consistent with the soon-to-be introduced idea of a "student personnel point of view" in higher education.

There were other issues, and certainly those touched upon above were far more complex than reported here. The intent of these remarks is simply to emphasize the separate emergence of the personnel worker. From the beginning, these persons used the tools of science and humanistic learning to the extent that the tools were available, adapting them to the needs of the student.

The growth of services has continued nearly unabated; by 1977, the American Personnel and Guidance Association reported 11 divisions of professional interest and a membership exceeding 41,000. If one were to subtract one division from the total, those affiliated principally with the

American College Personnel Association, few deans would be found in APGA. Other professional groups with a background related to the early days of student personnel have branched out into full-fledged national associations. Some of their numbers today report to a chief student personnel officer, but others do not. One sign of success, size, has inherent problems complete with diverse goals, practices, jargon, and specialized tools. *Some see this diversity as wholly understandable, a natural outcome of specialized interests, but others see it as evidence that the field has lost its compass.*

An entirely different story relates how the dean of students' position emerged as the principal personnel office on the American college campus. It is clear that the development of the new position was tied to campus territorial conflicts concerning the management of expanding services. In a general sense, the deans of women and deans of men were outflanked in these conflicts, because the broader services provided by the student personnel worker commanded more territory.

The deans of men and deans of women had relied heavily on the force of their personalities, and their reputations as effective teachers, in their work as deans. They held no special corner on administrative skills. The personnel workers tended to approach their work more scientifically and typically denied any administrative role. Nonetheless, they all sought to serve the same clientele. The inevitable conflict surfaced, resulting in some fundamental changes.

The dean of students' position was established to bring some order out of the substantial overlapping which resulted on some campuses. Persons with administrative skills were hired to direct the various staff and offices involved in working with students outside the classroom. Similarly, the notion of a campus "environment" began to emerge, resulting in organized planning and programs that were more comprehensive than the one-to-one delivery of services characteristic of the early period of our history.

The growth of the dean of students' position ushered in some subtle changes in the field. The leader was no longer (necessarily) an inspirational figure, but was more likely selected for his/her ability to develop or manage a variety of programs and services in behalf of students. *After losing the battle to the personnel worker, the dean of men frequently won the war by moving up to the dean of students' position.* This created additional problems, some of which are recognizable to the present time, as evidenced by the organizational arrangements of student personnel programs on individual campuses. The full impact of this benchmark change in our field, however, has yet to be explored.

*Writers have been fond of referring to our role as disciplinarians and as paternalistic figures.* These two labels have frequently resulted in unproductive embarrassment, chagrin, apology, and other responses. The observations seem as apt to come from those inside the field as outside, again suggesting limited historical understanding. It is not necessary to justify old behaviors as appropriate to the present, but it may be useful to consider the periods and circumstances in which these behaviors once had meaning. It may also be possible to show that the language we use to describe these old behaviors is one-dimensional, enhancing clarity but eroding accuracy. *A clearly understood distortion is a poor substitute for comprehending the complex circumstances that challenge our understanding. The choice seems fairly clear to this writer: Either we try to retreat from a past that we think we understand or we take a critical if uncomfortable look backward.* This will require a comprehensive approach on the part of future writers; the brief sections that follow are simply illustrative of the issues that should be resolved.

## Discipline

The subject of discipline has been one of the most pervasive and painful topics in the history of student personnel administration. Where it exists as a function of a student affairs office today, it is likely that structure and procedure dominate philosophy as matters for attention. This is understandable in view of recent court decisions. It might have been avoidable, but for excessive concern over "image" on our part.

From the beginning of our history, discipline has had several connotations. Three definitions are offered here: (1) discipline as a virtue, in other words self-discipline, the essence of education; (2) discipline as a process, a form or reeducation or rehabilitation; (3) discipline as punishment, typically seen as having redemptive features even in this narrow construction. Fley (1963) has conducted an excellent, comprehensive analysis of these features of discipline, a model historical study.

The first two definitions occupied most of the time and attention of the early deans, yet they are largely remembered for the third definition. Whatever the facts, "dean and discipline" are an integrated historical legacy. Barry and Wolf (1963), who have developed one of the few excellent historical overviews of the field, say of discipline: *"Despite all their later disclaimers, most deans of men seem to have been appointed primarily to act as disciplinarians."* (They did not say "were appointed," but the qualifying feature of the sentence might well be missed.) Fley (1963) notes, "The denial of the disciplinary function in student personnel work has resulted not so much from solid educational theories, as from a belief on the part of the present-day personnel worker that his predecessors in the field were snooping, petty battle-axes who made it their business to ferret out wickedness and punish all offenders promptly." The power of accepted history prevails, even though it is demonstrably inadequate.

The deans of men and deans of women dealing with "discipline" had distinctly different problems, and they are treated separately here.

Marion Talbot, one of the most influential early deans, and a founder of the Association of Collegiate Alumnae (later to be known as the American Association of University Women) gave "discipline" a broad construction (1898):

> It must not be limited to the mental powers—accuracy, agility, firmness and cleanness of mind and keeness of observation—it often does and always should include the training of the moral powers—truth, honor, justice, forbearance, self-control, patience, and reverence. Indeed, there can be no longer nor better aim for all educational effort than such all-inclusive discipline, and I believe that it not only now exists, but is growing to be more and more the chief end of training during the years with which we are dealing.

Talbot's statement is representative of the broad view of discipline. She saw it as "unlocking the virtues found in every student," a humanist position discussed in a later section of this chapter. Many deans of women offered comments in this vein.

One must eventually move from statements of ideals, however, to the essentials of practice. The deans of women, of course, were faced with responding to the apprehensions of their male colleagues with respect to women students. They were seen by some as potentially corrupting or corruptible, and there was concern about their health, state of mind, and general ability to cope in the collegiate setting. It was impossible for the deans of women to ignore these concerns. One reality was clear, as indicated by an early dean. "Indiscretion and folly meant a far bitterer repentance for one sex than the other . . ." (Matthews, 1915). No doubt the deans of women were eager to avoid any problems that would give credence to the view that women did not belong in these institutions. If they took a no-nonsense approach, it was likely because they had high moral standards, and because diversions cost them time and energy best spent elsewhere.

Fley (1963) notes that the deans of women rarely referred to "discipline" in their proceedings, choosing instead words such as "character formation," "moral and ethical training," and "citizenship training." It was impossible for them to fend off the role of "discipline," but in accepting it they were able to attempt to cast this responsibility in ways *they* deemed appropriate. The issue was a difficult but not a central concern. Simply put, they sought to enlarge the career and leadership opportunities of women, and they recognized competence as crucial. Nowhere in the written word is punishment, the third view of discipline, found in the thinking of these women. Every cute story (e.g., the enforcement of a rule requiring a magazine be placed under any young woman sitting on someone's lap), cruelly discredits the remarkable work of a group of remarkable women.

Deans of men had their definitions, and faced their own set of conditions and expectations, and their struggle with the concept is duly recorded. The deans of women either suffered in silence or took an oblique view, but the deans of men were more verbal and more straightforward. Some of them accepted the responsibility, taking the view in behavior situations that positive relationships could grow out of negative beginnings. Others were not so sanguine. As one dean put it, "Discipline is about as welcome as a cow-bird in a cuckoo's nest."

The deans of men saw increasing discipline problems on the campus and pressed for the reasons. Many talked about the aftermath of war (World War I) and the general breakdown in values in the larger society following it. The representative of another group observed that it was more pressing, "in direct . . . proportion as the curriculum has become more illogical or superficial" (Secretarial Notes, 1927). They possessed the same high ideals and moral standards that characterized the early deans of women, and the crisis of values perceived in American society was profoundly disturbing to many of them.

The longstanding assumption that moralizing, exhortation, or threat were the principal tools of the deans of men could not be substantiated by this writer. Additionally, any joy in meting out punishment is totally absent in the *Proceedings* of either the deans of men or women in those times.

Some of the statements attributed to the deans could, on the one hand, be characterized as paternalistic; a broader view might favor a kind of *noblesse oblige* approach, wholly in keeping with their own high ideals. Dean Stanley Coulter of Purdue offered one perspective:

> Unless the Dean of Men . . . is something of a practical idealist of youth . . . unless he is all consumed with a passion of love for young people, his work is nothing. The biggest job I have is not the control of delinquents, it is not the control of ordinary misconduct, but in doing and living so well, showing the individual his powers and how with the right use of those powers he can live a life of honor or how he can waste all these inheritances. (Secretarial Notes, 1928)

Many of the deans of men were faced with enforcing rules established by the faculty, and it is clear that this was an odious assignment. If ample records were available, they might well show the dean of men as "subverter" rather than "enforcer." They were required to finesse their way through the turmoil created by rules that generally lagged behind the prevailing attitudes and behaviors of young people. This was an extraordinary task, requiring unique styles of response, but today many in the field underestimate these early challenges, or simply distort them through superficial attention.

Robert Reinow, the University of Iowa's first dean of men, was clearly angry about the situation he faced, as the following passage reveals:

> . . . it is plain to see that our worn-out system of traditional discipline, our enforcement of faculty-made regulations, are futile. They are not constructive; they are not inspiring; they are not educational. They were never intended as such. They are, and have been, a sort of protective measure established by the faculties to maintain a decent awe and respect in the number of students with a fear of the consequences that might follow violation of the same. (Secretarial Notes, 1929)

Yet he observed that somehow during college the ideals of life, of conduct, of behavior, and of self-discipline must be developed.

There are many additional aspects of the concept of "discipline" in this century. Some key people who initially felt it to be inimical to the field later changed their minds. Prominent among these were E.G. Williamson and Esther Lloyd-Jones. Fley believes that the statement on self-discipline by Lloyd-Jones and her colleague, Margaret Ruth Smith, to be one of the finest in the literature (Lloyd-Jones, 1938). Perhaps the most supportive analytical treatment of the subject was written by another early critic,

E.G. Williamson, who collaborated with J.D. Foley in *Counseling and Discipline*, published in 1949. Fritz Redl introduced the idea of group work in discipline, in 1947.

Carl Rogers had problems with the idea of discipline, making one of the strongest cases against it in noting, "Therapy and authority cannot be co-existent in the same relationship," but "yet . . . mere leniency is not the answer." (Rogers, 1942) He offered some alternatives, but his reservations have been persuasive to many in the field.

Why has this issue been of such importance to the field? The "control of behavior" theme has been a vocal interpretation of the question, but it is incomplete. The question is deeply philosophical; there are writers who have recognized it as such, but their numbers are small. The Athenians believed that values could be taught, and must be taught. Centuries later, John Dewey would write: "Restoring integration and cooperation between man's beliefs about the world in which he lives and his beliefs about the values and purposes that should direct his conduct is the deepest problem of human life."

Dewey's words may seem obscure today, but they reflect the attitudes of the early deans, who brought high ideals, well-defined values, and a strong moral sense to their work. These traits governed their work and were transmitted to their students. What was once a virtue has become the opposite, an observation not inconsistent with Eric Fromm's views in *The Sane Society* (1955). The prevailing judgment we have of these deans tends to be unsympathetic, but we may have it backward.

## In Loco Parentis

The concept of *in loco parentis* is another educational household word glibly used but incompletely understood. It illustrates how events relevant at a given point in time can take on meanings later that are only loosely related to the origins from which they stemmed. Modern student personnel workers have cringed at the thought of being party to the concept of *in loco parentis*.

There are at least two ironies in the concept of *in loco parentis*. First, it is a legal doctrine not an educational statement, and its formalization into law occurred long after the original relationship was abandoned in practice. Second, it is a doctrine that has come to characterize much of student personnel work, but its legal application referred almost entirely to matters of student discipline, which at the time were generated by rules developed and enforced by faculty members. *Far from rebutting the issue, our profession meekly accepted its tenets and was apologetic thereafter. The price of neglecting a rebuttal has been so high that it appears beyond repair.*

The preponderance of writers describing the relationships between student and institution in colonial America refer to *in loco parentis.* (They also borrowed the term from the courts, applying the nomenclature retroactively.) The relationship, to the extent that it did exist, was understandable, given the age of students and the difficulties associated with travel and communication during the colonial period. *In loco parentis,* however, probably misstates the case. Certainly it is doubtful that colonial college faculty ever thought of the matter that way. This is a matter for other researchers, but this writer feels that the relationship was moral, in religious terms, a deeper concern than simply serving as surrogate parents, which the college also did. Rudolph (1976) leans this way in noting that *the souls of these students were what the college felt was at stake.* If this produces chuckles in our modern age, *we can be sobered in realizing that, in the view of Jacob (1957), institutions may be making few value-oriented contributions to their students.*

It is clear in any case that the relationship of student and institution changed with the rise of the public university. The institution might indeed have felt a relationship with students like that of the colonial college, but it simply did not exist. Thus, while the *facts* of this relationship changed, a strong residual tradition remained. In the last decades of the nineteenth century, the neglect of student life was a growing phenomenon, and any characterization of higher education having a parental relationship distorts the matter completely.

The approach to the relationship might well have been argued to be *educational,* entailing the view that an institution should have, within the bounds of fairness, the inherent power to establish regulations in its own behalf. The notion of inherent power did surface but never took hold. The case for an educational relationship had some spotted success, but its potential is fast disappearing.

It is regrettable that the Gott court (which introduced the language of *in loco parentis* in 1913) did not reach a decision on the basis of an earlier case, Hill vs. McCauley, recorded in 1887. Much of the "due process" frame of reference found in the landmark case of Dixon vs. Alabama State

Board of Education (in 1961) rests in the decision rendered in Hill vs. McCauley. The Hill decision noted, "The dismissal of students from college should be in accordance with those principles of justice. . . which are recognized as controlling in the determination of the rights of men in every civilized nation on the globe" (Cazier, 1973). Certainly this is true, and we should be none the poorer for having to comply with the "due process" procedures outlined in Dixon vs. Alabama State Board of Education. None of these early cases, however, involved student personnel administrators. Yet from the specific case of discipline, which became a student personnel function, developed the notion of "parental" which spread across the profession in an interesting manifestation of guilt by inference. The fact that the "parental" case has never been made is an inconvenient irritation long since fallen by the wayside. Certainly we can take no pride in instances of capricious treatment on the part of student personnel officers, and just as certainly students do not give up their basic rights once they enter the campus. The growing body of law applied to higher education, however, relies on analogy, and every case provides a precedent for yet another case. This introduces the risk of administrators' dwelling on procedures rather than upon the substantive personal or educational issues they face with respect to problems of student behavior. A new surrogate parent is on the horizon, with muscle few parents ever had, and the "parent" is looking at higher educational institutions, not the student. This writer recalls the admonition of Learned Hand: "A society so riven that the spirit of moderation is gone, no court can save; . . . in a society which evades its responsibility by thrusting upon the courts the nurture of that spirit, that spirit will surely perish."

We have failed to address an inaccurate analogy applied to us unfairly. This has resulted in a one-dimensional view of discipline. Our chances of countering the view seem slim indeed.

One last lament will close this section. A parental relationship, if the analogy holds, could well involve love, mutual respect, and certainly a concern for a student's growth and development. This aspect of the argument must be absurd, for no one has given it any attention.

## Values in Historical Perspective

The early deans in the field were deeply concerned about values, though they are remembered best as "moralizers" rather than as "moral."

And yet, fifty years and more later, the APGA national award for outstanding research (1976) dealt with moral education. V. Lois Erickson, the winner of the award, notes: "There are many kinds of values, and moral values are only one of them . . . but moral development involves restructuring empathy and issues of justice to lead to a greater good for more people." This observation reflects the same kind of ideals espoused by our predecessors and bears upon the style they brought to their work.

Is it important at all for us to consider that we are still concerned about the basic human issues that were discussed by the early deans? It is at least an arguable point that the major difference between the field then and today, is the eighty or so years of experience that they lacked.

It is clear that in every age thoughtful men and women have pondered over value issues; that is evident in every enduring piece of literature written about human dilemmas. In the following paragraphs, this writer hopes to suggest some value issues outside the field of student personnel that have influenced our work, because their influence pervades our culture. They are suggestive of the ways we make choices, the ways our predecessors made choices, indeed the ways such choices were *allowed* to be made in the face of powerful cultural forces.

There are dozens of definitions of the word "value," some of them understandable and others less clear. The definition offered by W.H. Cowley (1966) is adequate for purposes of this chapter: "A value constitutes a subjective attitude of a human individual or group at a given point in time and space about the worth of any objective, projective, or subjective entity."

Note the notion of "subjective," as it can be argued that no entity has value in itself. Note also the reference to time and space, a critical flaw in the informal history we have come to accept in student personnel administration. Note also that values are not ideals, though there can be ideal values. This is not double-talk; it means that ideals are positive, while values can be positive or negative (or something else). It is recognized, of course, that, in combination, one acquires a set of values resulting in a personal value system. This is a crucial matter; through it one transcends momentary pain and pleasure, enabling one to coordinate a virtually unlimited number of experiences encompassing the whole of one's life.

Our interests are not only concerned with the content of values, but also the way in which they are acquired, and the way in which they are held, their *salience* with regard to self-appraisal and ultimate behavior; for values imply choices made or not made, deeds done or not done, enjoyments experienced or not experienced, etc., ad infinitum.

And of course we don't live alone. The way in which a society, or any segment of that society, behaves is a product of values. Culture, or society, can be seen as a system of consensually validated social expectations derived from the personal values of diverse individuals. Cultural sanctions and expectations take on "good" and "bad" connotations, then , which are frequently referred to as morals. It is hoped that this thin introduction to sociology is not new to the reader, but simply a reminder of the ways we have operated in the varying milieus of our time.

A glimpse of some of these historical forces is all that can be offered here. No special claim is made for them, except that they need more examination than they have received from other authors and more than they will receive here.

The first of these forces is *humanism*. Originating in the Renaissance and gaining its full stature during the European Age of Reason, its vital values are: (1) a belief in human rationality; (2) confidence in the possibility of human perfectibility; (3) a recognition of the importance of self-awareness. One will immediately recognize our debt to these concepts.

It should not be necessary to indicate the importance of humanism in American history, as the historical humanists were especially persuasive to Thomas Jefferson and James Madison, the principal architects of our system of government.

During the nineteenth century, humanism took on some decidedly American pragmatic qualities. Reason, it was averred, should result in action, and reason and achievement became joined in ways unique to the American nation. Its existence coincided with the growth of our industrial nation, and for a time the two continued side by side. As the American frontier closed and people were thrown into close contact in the country's growing cities, the unfettered enthusiasm for men's right to achieve began to wane. The exploitation of immigrant workers, women, and children began to cast doubt on the virtue of unbridled individualism; the humanists faced some problems that they are still pondering. They faced these problems in higher education toward the end of the nineteenth century.

The second humanist value is the actualization of one's inner potential. As Marshall Lowe (1969) puts it, "Humanists continue to emphasize individual initiative and to believe in progress and in man's ability to perfect his world." It is in this second humanistic value that the notion of achievement sets its deepest roots. As a matter of fact, human achievement yokes the idea of rationality with the concept of self, of self-awareness.

Attention to the third tenet of humanism, that of self-awareness, characterizes our field. As far back as William James, we are introduced to the concept of self in a specific psychological sense; even Emerson once said, "This thought which is called I."

The notion of a self-concept has broadened to the point that it has many variations in psychological usage. Perhaps the case is made best by Abraham Maslow, who gave us the concept of self-actualization, which the humanists would see as the highest good. Carl Rogers made this point in the 1950s. A positive regard for oneself is so important, according to Rogers, that he wrote an entire book, *Client-Centered Therapy*, about it in 1951. That title-phrase is certainly a household word for those in our profession who come from counseling backgrounds. The views he sets down are those of the classical humanist: failing in self-awareness, in a concept of self, individuals encounter deficiencies and difficult adjustments that must be corrected if they are to have a productive life. The goal of therapy was to expand self-awareness. He saw this effort as a process, a direction, not a destination, but it was a *crucial* process.

Perhaps the most powerful and enduring American humanist is Erich Fromm. While arguing for the self in *Escape From Freedom* (1941), Fromm notes that the price of individual freedom may be too high for many, resulting in loneliness and isolation. He was deeply concerned with the persuasive reasons that could be developed for conforming to more dominant voices. This view was expanded six years later in *Man For Himself*, in which Fromm created the phrase "marketing orientation" as a fearful trend in American society. Here the self must conform and please in order to get along, a function, he thought, of the marketing orientation of an industrial society inappropriately applied to individuals. This assertion is still sound; a fear of group rejection is a *paramount* human concern, a pervasive anxiety of our time. In *The Sane Society*, perhaps Fromm's best work, written in 1955, he observed that our society is well on the path to replacing virtue with vice.

In summary, humanists are basically optimistic; they embrace reason, perfectibility, and self-awareness as their human imperatives. These values were the stock-in-trade of the early deans. A thoughtful writer needs to examine their status today.

In higher education, the humanistic orientation of higher education was weakened by an influx of teachers with an allegiance to science, an *empirically* schooled professoriate which embraced the principles of what has come to be called "the scientific method." In its human sense, it sought to measure experience through the senses. Because values cannot be perceived in this way, the empiricist is tempted to avoid the dilemma altogether, leaving the matter to indirection. The empiricists hoped to achieve through science an understanding of self that had failed in philosophy.

In psychology, Freud was the first dominant figure, the first to use a scientific medical model in examining human problems. Our field has fastened onto the tool of science now known as behaviorism. The prevailing view is that behaviorism is a rejection of humanism; having lost confidence in reason as a sufficient device, the behaviorist chose to encounter human problems through scientific observation and experimentation. Its building-block approach has achieved some spectacular results, but its basic weakness lies in the thorny questions of goals and purposes. One should be quick to point out that behaviorism is not "anti-human." Behaviorists simply hold the view that their work is a corrective to the failure they see in classical humanism.

The last historical force noted in this brief section is existentialism. Rollo May has observed that it is an attempt to resolve the "reason" and "science" cleavage that has characterized Western thought, moving away from a view of humans in the subject-object terms of humanism and behaviorism. The boundaries of existentialism are not yet fully understood, but Paul Tillich believed existentialism to be the prevailing intellectual force of our time. A complex phenomenon, it has been seen by Max Wise (1966) as having four characteristics that are helpful to understanding:

1. It is a protest against the assumption that reality can be grasped primarily or exclusively by intellectual means.

2. It is a protest against the view which regards men as "things," as assortments of functions and reactions. It stands against naturalism (of which behaviorism is a part) and mechanism.

3. It makes a drastic distinction between subjective and objective truth and gives priority to the subjective. This means, not the denial of objective truth, but a denial of its adequacy on matters of ultimate concern, which are always dealt with by the person.

4. It regards man as fundamentally ambiguous; he is free to act, yet he is enmeshed in the natural and social order. He is finite, yet he can on occasion rise above any situation. He is bounded by time, yet he has a kinship with eternity.

In the *Courage to Be* (1952), Paul Tillich identifies World War I as the crucial point for the onset of sustained existentialist thought, although it is a much older philosophy. During World War I, old beliefs in the inevitability of human progress and the rationality of human thought were shattered, particularly in Europe but with considerable force in this country as well. Rollo May describes the movement as a response to the increasing fragmentation and compartmentalization of personality, a function of industrialized society, factors sensed but not fully understood by the early deans.

Existentialism represents a search for new moral values; it is a quest for personal meaning. It has declared war on older, conventional values; certainly that is its hallmark. It has both theistic and atheistic features, but they are not differentiated in this brief discussion.

In many respects, existentialism is a philosophy of anxiety, though its American version is more optimistic than its European counterpart. It stresses the development of self through intense inwardness, our modern hope of keeping or regaining an individualism opposed by technological society. One will note the similarities here with humanism, but the principal battle is not based primarily in reason; it is between being and non-being. Non-being, for purposes here, can be considered as the constant threat of personal and social annihilation, an unrelenting battle. The greatest fear is man as object, according to Sartre. While Sartre describes the necessity of the freedom to be (through negation), Tillich turns to the courage to be through the affirmation of self. Carl Roger's book, *On Becoming A person* (1961), has a distinctive, American existential feeling to it.

It is no doubt true that these schools of thinking do not arrange themselves as neatly in our lives and work as they are set out here. But neither are they simply interesting abstractions. Indeed, they are forces that are influencing us whether we know it or not. But how? This writer has found few persons with the capacity or interest to adapt the thinking inherent in these philosophies (and no doubt other philosophies) to our work. An important contribution to the field can be made by persons willing to examine and present these issues.

It can be argued that the press for "student development" is grounded in one or more of these philosophies. The available literature, however, is strong in technique and weak in philosophy. It is clear that there is a "student personnel point of view." But the statements of philosophy that are affecting modern civilization and to which that "point of view" is tied are worthy of more thoughtful analysis.

This is a drama without end; but clearer perspectives are needed. If we understand the need for mutuality, affiliation, and community with other human beings, we at least have some things to talk about. If it seems depressing, we can take hope in noting that men and women have shown resilience in facing all of these problems, beyond that recognized by many writers. A central question is whether society needs a center of meaning to give it the coherence necessary for the quality of life its members are seeking, or whether a personal center of meaning is possible and then sufficient enough to provide the stability necessary for persons having broadly diverse goals and values. This is an on-going dilemma found on nearly every campus.

## Historical Writing

Before closing this chapter, it would seem appropriate to note some issues that have a bearing on historical writing. These are not just abstractions; they influence the way we come to view ourselves.

In looking at the study of history, one may fail to note how complex and forbidding it tends to be. Lay persons typically see it as involving the location, digestion, and interpretation of sources found in places where historians ordinarily look. It may be surprising to those who have not had the opportunity, nor the interest in pursuing the matter, to learn that historians suffer many professional problems and divisions. This writer could not help but observe that many of these problems and divisions also mirror those in the field of student personnel administration.

Historians have been at their work longer, of course, but they are still arguing epistemological questions. They constantly haggle over terms and definitions and face astonishing semantic problems in general. The impact of the "scientific method" has troubled them throughout this century. They approach their work with a variety of prejudices and sentiments. They understand human behavior incompletely. They must rely heavily on fair-minded, professional judgments in order to draw conclusions. Some methods and formulations they desperately need are simply not available to them. Finally, as one historian put it, "Historians . . . have to accept much knowledge on trust" (Renier, 1965).

Historians are typically forced to confront the uncontrolled and merciless evidence of the written word. This presents for them the problem of *context.* To identify an isolated issue is not sufficient; only an understanding of the surrounding circumstances will yield the meaning sought. It can be argued that any "issue" that ignores a larger context of cirumstances may well not be the "issue" but something else entirely, or partially, with critical shadings and nuances. To miss some of these, and perhaps to focus inappropriately on others, is to illustrate the difficult problems historians must resolve if they are to give their work value. It is the connectedness of the events that brings meaning to the best historical writing, an art of the highest order.

Even *words, terms, and/or phrases* understood when spoken or written in a given period may become misleading and/or useless as their meanings change over time. Certainly this is well understood in theory, but violations of the theory in practice are evident in the writing available to us. "Moral," "citizenship," "character development," "adjustment," and the "whole student" illustrate this point—words once understood may have had different connotations at that time than they now have.

Similarly, words used at any one point in time may take on different meanings. In our field, "discipline" would be one such word; the meaning of "discipline" has perhaps caused more consternation in our field than has any other single word, yet it has had concurrent meanings. "Student development" may be a phrase which future writers will find puzzling, frustrating.

Historical writing is a cumulative venture, like most other intellectual disciplines in which scholars rely heavily on the good work of their predecessors. It is obvious, of course, why this is so, lest every historical writer have to return to primary source material found all over the globe. *Accepted history* or *accepted sources,* then, are valuable tools for the historian. They emerge from the quality of care and scholarship which later writers see in a predecessor's efforts. The principal risk of accepted history is that it may become invulnerable to challenge. (It must be noted that this is not so much a problem for professional historians as it is for lay persons like ourselves, who are apt to assume that our accepted history must be accurate.) Student personnel administrators have failed to challenge the accepted history of the field, writing that for the most part was set out a quarter of a century or more ago, and which has been tested only indifferently, if at all, since. Certainly we do not want to create any new myths, but just as surely we must question many. We have dehumanized our predecessors through basic ignorance, writing them off as "paternalistic" or "disciplinarians" or suffering other unhappy fates, principally because we have been indifferent historians in our own field.

Consider the following example, an illustration of stereotyped thinking and writing; the authors' names are omitted to eliminate any possible embarrassment.

> One of the historical models for the student personnel worker is that of regulator or repressor. The student personnel profession came into being largely because the president needed help in regulating student behavior. In the early 1900s student personnel workers were given the titles of 'monitor' and 'warden.'

> In this model the student personnel regulator works on colonial campuses as a mercenary of the president at war with students. He is the president's *no-man*. He tends to behave in ways that regulate, repress, reject, reproof, reprimand, rebuff, rebuke, reserve, reduce, and even remove human potential. In this system all the negative aspects of *in loco parentis* are practiced as staff members attempt to maintain a strict supervision over the affairs of students.

If the profession deserves this bitter pill, then certainly it should work to recover from such a harmful, negative beginning. But the concern here is that the book from which this material is quoted, a book written principally for community college administrators, may become part of our accepted history. (This has already happened, in the judgment of this writer, though the severity of this material is unparalleled elsewhere.) As such, other writers may draw upon this reference as an accurate description. It may be useful to look more carefully at these two paragraphs, to ask some reasonable questions, and to make some general observations.

1. **What citations are provided to verify the several assertions of the writers?** None.

2. **Why are the references absent?** Because no primary materials exist that would support these views. Careful investigation will inevitably reach this conclusion.

3. **What evidence exists to indicate that the "president needed help" in regulating student behavior?** This is a partial truth, but void of any of the several nuances it deserves. If anything, this might have been more true of the role of deans of women, but even this statement by itself is inadequate. The best test of this statement is found in early *Proceedings* of the deans of men and of women. Their view of their responsibilities, and their behavior on the job, adequately rebuts the simplistic view of the authors. The authors' position is principally incorrect *by itself*, by what it ignores.

4. **"In the early 1900s student personnel workers were given the titles of 'monitor' and 'warden.'"** This is a factual misstatement, but even if it were not, one might say, "so what?" Today they are called vice presidents! A denigrating interpretation of the title monitor and warden in the 1970s is useless, aside from the fact that they had disappeared by the early 1900s.

5. **"In this model the student personnel regulator works on colonial campuses . . . "** The last referent was to the 1900s, so the reader is left with an abrupt and confusing transition. The colonial reference, of course, is ludicrous. There were no personnel workers on the colonial campus (Leonard, 1955). Any antecedent personnel services that existed in the colonial college were performed by the president and the teaching faculty. It seems unjustified that we would have to accept responsibility for the behavior of the faculty of the colonial college, even without conceding that the behavior of these colonial figures was inappropriate to their circumstances.

6. **The faculty of the colonial college had a clear frame of reference, highly moral, with a kinship to the Puritan views of the period, with all that implies.** The authors show no evidence of appreciating or understanding the differing motivations and values of historical periods. The sneering in the two quoted paragraphs obviously implies that we are in much better shape today. It is an arguable point; we aren't interested in souls any longer, because we aren't sure there is any such thing. It probably follows that we would not appreciate those for whom this was a preeminent concern.

7.  **Note the reference to** *in loco parentis.* This is a legal term which did not find its way into higher education until the twentieth century. It was meant to apply to the entire collegiate system, not to student personnel work. One would suspect that the 14-year-old boys attending the colonial college probably did need some careful guidance. The important point here is that the college viewed itself as wholly responsible for these young boys (no girls, of course) and applying a twentieth century term to a complex set of concerns occurring a hundred years (and more) earlier is wholly unjustified.

8.  **"He is the president's no-man."** One must glumly conclude here that the authors consulted none of the early deans' *Proceedings* readily available.

9.  **In the period that spawned the creation and development of the field of student personnel administration, any number of factors existed, as indicated earlier in this chapter. The authors have simply ignored them all.**

10. **Perhaps the most revealing feature of the two paragraphs is the seventeen pejorative words contained therein, written no doubt for purposes of alliteration, but wholly void of fairness.** We find here that our predecessors sought even to "remove human potential." How believable is this assertion, even in common-sense terms?

It seems only fair to consider the authors' possible rebuttal to these comments, had they been given the opportunity. They might point out that the "model" does not necessarily refer to the later practices stemming from it. It seems clear, however, that the authors' views of the behavior of deans of the early 1900s were patterned on the model. This is an associationistic approach, and certainly the approach is valid. The argument, however, is one of content. Simply to note the "B" behavior follows from "A" behavior does not excuse the critical factor of evidence. (The laws of association date back to Aristotle!)

Why should time be spent in such an extensive rebuttal of two small paragraphs? It is important because one is not sure what impact these paragraphs will have as a written legacy. The rebuttal illustrates how difficult it would be for any of us to closely examine the written material to which we are exposed. Typically, we do not have the background, nor certainly the time, to scrutinize in depth all that we read. Although we read questioningly, we must depend upon the credibility of writers. We must able to trust the *care* with which writers approach their work. Readers have to contend with errors of fact and problems of interpretation; it is hoped that they can avoid having to be suspicious of prejudicial work. Every writer must work to minimize this suspicion, moving the reader to the real issues under discussion.

A last example of the dilemma of historical writing is the phenomenon of *revision*. This is not a rewriting of the truth but an examination of what was genuinely thought to be true in the face of new evidence. Revision must always be held as a clear possibility in historical writing. Even long-standing assumptions should be vulnerable as new writing and thinking emerge. John Dewey once observed that as new material is developed, it will always be at the mercy of the discoveries which made it possible. Historically speaking, our field has no new materials; worse, we have not made good use of the material which already exists.

Without exception, historians must face all of the issues outlined here; they are as much a part of the discipline as are the tentative judgments that eventually find their way to the printed page. The struggle to overcome these limitations is the essence of historical writing. The accumulated successes of historians represent one major contribution to modern civilization. Our profession apparently has chosen to ignore the struggle. Our graduate schools, with some notable exceptions, have failed to prepare emerging student personnel professionals either with the tools of historical research or with an appreciation of the worth of historical understanding.

## In Summary

Any number of topical issues could have been treated historically in this chapter—a practice not common in our literature. This writer has attempted to indicate a few of these issues that have had a particularly important impact on the profession, and to suggest that the myths which surround these issues have resulted in legacies which have been harmful in some instances to our self-perception and the views others have of us.

It will be necessary for future writers to research questions bearing upon the field, to see what kind of myths remain in our midst. Once new interpretations are made and reported, they will be used again, contributing to an *accepted history* that is different from present views. This may take much time, and many contributors, but until it is done the student affairs practitioner will remain cut off from the past, or will suffer from a past that never existed at all, but is believed, nonetheless.

# References

Barry, R. and Wolf, B. *Modern Issues in Guidance-Personnel Work.* New York: Teachers College, Columbia University, 1963.

Bathurst, J.E. What is Student Personnel Work? *Educational Record,* 1938, 19, 502-515.

Birenbaum, W.M. The State of the Art. In T.F. Harrington, *Student Personnel Work in Urban Colleges.* New York: Intext Educational Publishers, 1974, 145-181.

Blackburn, J.L. Perceived Purposes of Student Personnel Programs by Chief Student Personnel Officers as a Function of Academic Preparation and Experience. Unpublished doctoral dissertation, Florida State University, 1969.

Blaesser, W.W. The Contributions of the American Council on Education to Student Personnel Work in Higher Education. Unpublished doctoral dissertation, George Washington University, 1953.

Boring, E.G. *A History of Experimental Psychology.* New York: Appleton, 1950.

Brewer, J.M. *History of Vocational Guidance.* New York: Harper and Brothers, 1942.

Brown, R.D. *Student Development in Tomorrow's Higher Education: A Return to the Academy.* Monograph No. 16, The American College Personnel Association, 1972.

Brubacher, J.S. and Rudy, W. *Higher Education in Transition.* New York: Harper and Row, 1968.

Callis, R. Educational Aspects of *In Loco Parentis. Journal of College Student Personnel,* 1967, 8, 231-234.

Cazier, S. *Student Discipline Systems in Higher Education,* (ERIC higher education research report no. 7). Washington, D.C.: American Association for Higher Education, 1973.

Cook, Barbara I. Sixty Years and Beyond. *Journal of the National Association for Women Deans, Administrators, and Counselors,* 1976, 39, 196-204.

Cowley, W.H. The History and Philosophy of Student Personnel Work. *Journal of the National Association of Deans of Women*, 1940, 3, 153-162.

Cowley, W.H. A Holistic Overview of American Colleges and Universities. Mimeographed, 1966, 69-86.

Crookston, B.B. An Organizational Model for Student Development. *Journal of the National Association of Student Personnel Administrators*, 1972, 10, 3-13.

Duricka, P. Moral Development: Restructuring Values. *APGA Guidepost*, May 13, 1976, 18 (1), 4.

Fley, J. Discipline in Student Personnel Work: The Changing Views of Deans and Personnel Workers. Unpublished doctoral dissertation, University of Illinois, 1963.

Fromm, E. *Escape from Freedom.* New York: Farrar and Rinehart, Inc., 1941.

Fromm, E. *Man for Himself.* Greenwich, Connecticut: Fawcett Publications, 1947.

Fromm, E. *The Sane Society.* New York: Rinehart, 1955.

Heath, K.G. Our Heritage Speaks. *Journal of the National Association for Women Deans, Administrators, and Counselors*, 1976, 39, 90-97.

Holmes, L. *A History of the Position of Dean of Women in a Selected Group of Co-educational Colleges and Universities in the United States.* New York: Teachers College, Columbia University, 1939.

Jacob, P.E. *Changing Values in College.* New York: Harper and Brothers, 1957.

Laudicina, R. and Tramutola, J.L. *A Legal Perspective for Student Personnel Administrators.* Springfield, Illinois: Charles C. Thomas, 1974.

Leonard, E.A. Origins of Personnel Services in American Higher Education. Minneapolis: University of Minnesota Press, 1956.

Lloyd-Jones, E.M. and Smith, M.R. *A Student Personnel Program for Higher Education.* New York and London: McGraw-Hill, 1938.

Lowe, C.M. *Value Orientations in Counseling and Psychotherapy.* San Francisco: Chandler Company, 1969.

Mathews, L.K. *The Dean of Women.* Boston: Houghton Mifflin Company, 1915.

Moore, Paul. An Analysis of the Position of Dean of Students in Selected Institutions of Higher Education. Unpublished Dissertation, The University of Southern California, 1977.

Murphy, G. *Historical Introduction to Modern Psychology.* New York: Harcourt, Brace, 1949.

Nunn, N.L. Student Personnel Work in American Higher Education: Its Evolution as an Organized Movement. Unpublished doctoral dissertation, Florida State University, 1964.

O'Banion, T. and Thurston A. (Eds.) *Student Development Programs in the Community Junior College.* Englewood Cliffs, N.J.: Prentice Hall, Inc., 1972.

Penney, J.F. Student Personnel Work: A Profession Stillborn. *Personnel and Guidance Journal,* June 1969, 47, (10), 958-962.

Phillips, K.S. *My room in the World* (with Keith Jennison). New York, Abingdon, 1964.

Renier, G.J. *History: Its Purpose and Method.* New York: Harper and Row, 1965.

Rhatigan, J.J. History as a Potential Ally. *Journal of the National Association of Student Personnel Administrators,* 1974, 11, (3), 11-15.

Rhatigan, J.J. Student Services versus Student Development: Is There a Difference? *Journal of the National Association for Women Deans, Administrators, and Counselors,* 1975, 38 (2), 51-58.

Rogers, C.R. *Counseling and Psychotherapy.* New York: Houghton Mifflin Company, 1942.

Rogers, C.R. *Client-centered Therapy, its Current Practice, Implications, and Theory.* Boston: Houghton Mifflin Company, 1951.

Rogers, C.R. *On Becoming a Person; a Therapist's View of Psychotherapy.* Boston: Houghton Mifflin, 1961.

Rudolph, F. The American College Student: From Theologian to Technocrat in 300 Years. Mimeographed. An address to the fifty-eighth annual conference of the National Association of Student Personnel Administrators, April, 1976.

Secretarial notes on the annual conferences of deans and advisers of men of midwestern institutions. 1921; 1923; 1924; 1927; 1928; 1929; 1932.

Talbot, M. Journal of the Association of Collegiate Alumnae, Series III, No. 1, 1898, 25.

Tillich, P. *The Courage To Be.* New Haven: Yale University Press, 1952.

Vermilye, D.W. Student Development in Tomorrow's Higher Education: The Beginning of a Dialogue. *Journal of College Student Personnel,* 1973, 14, (1), 77-87.

Watson, J.B. *Behaviorism.* Chicago: The University of Chicago Press, fourth impression, 1962.

Williamson, E.G. and Foley, J.D. *Counseling and Discipline.* 1st ed. New York: McGraw-Hill, 1949.

Wise, M. Existentialism and Guidance-Personnel Work. *Journal of the National Association for Women Deans, Administrators, and Counselors,* 1976, 39, 196-204.

# On Deaning and Learning

ALTHOUGH AMERICAN HIGHER EDUCATION was an offspring of the English and Continental systems, it developed its own distinctive character and mission. It was similar to its counterparts in its intent to create, preserve, and transmit knowledge and extend human development through scholarship, research, instruction, and public service. It was, however, unique in its commitment to serve the needs of the American democratic society and its individual members, not just to educate the elite. The commitment has been to develop the talents of citizens so that they may perform effectively as individuals and also contribute to the corporate society. Moreover, a concern for the moral, spiritual, and physical welfare as well as the intellectual development of students has been woven into the fabric of American higher education.

If they threw us out tomorrow, an office would be created the next day to stop the dogs from barking during class.—Smith

This broader educational model resulted in programs and services which extended well beyond the classroom and laboratory. Then as facuties assumed research and public service missions in addition to teaching, as campuses grew and student bodies became more heterogeneous, student affairs deans and their colleagues assumed primary responsibility for this extension of the learning environment. The student affairs office became the agency that counseled and assisted students and built the campus programs to affirm the goal of full development of the individual learner. Of course, some services like residential accommodations and student health programs developed because they were essential when large groups of students were brought together and such programs were not available in the local community. Specialties such as admission services and financial aid emerged to meet new requirements; pressure from students and parents extended administrative control functions. A separate profession developed to meet the program needs and values which extended beyond the formal curriculum.

---

**The concern for the "whole" student is still important, as is the quality of campus life which is necessary to support this concept. The question is, what can we do to improve the quality of life for the learner?—Smith**

---

Student affairs developed in the United States as nowhere else in the world. Its uniqueness as a manifestation of American education is set forth in the preceding chapter; its function and purposes, integrated in the philosophy and purpose of higher education in American society, is considered in this chapter.

The dean grows weary of the trustee's inevitable concern reflected in the question, "Do you have the campus quiet today?," when the scope of the deans' mission has long since broadened. Student affairs staffs today view their roles as primarily educational, complementing the classroom, the library, the laboratory—the faculty—by providing opportunities for students to develop their talents through creative experiences, exchanges, and settings. In their optimum setting student affairs programs offer a full range of services and activities to meet the intellectual, personal, social, and interpersonal needs of students.

Yet, several key educational leaders and more than a few presidents are beginning to look askance at their student affairs colleagues and their programs. If the student affairs staffs are created to teach values and matters that faculty have not wanted to teach, and which are now either of lessening importance or represent areas reclaimed by the faculty, then why maintain student affairs programs? If we learned to be competent crisis managers in the 60s but crises are not a significant agenda today, what validity do we now have? If we exist primarily to insure that students arrive at classes and laboratories on time, in good health, and financially sound, couldn't other administrative units assume such functions? These questions represent more than hypothetical challenges to the highly developed student affairs programs that continue to function in the colleges and universities in this country.

Added to this are the budgetary constraints and a predicted drop in high school graduates available for admission to post-secondary education. Interest is peaked in reassessing the institutional mission and renewing concern among administrators over the retention of students. Do student affairs administrators play a part in this reassessment?

If student affairs programs did not exist in any form, would we reappear *de novo* and, if so, to do what? Regardless how organized, or under what administrative aegis, what can be affirmed about our mission? What assumptions may be stated about learning, campus environments, and the role of the student affairs dean in the learning process which help us in defining this mission, role, and even structure?

## Some Assumptions about Learning and Educational Environments

Before describing in more detail the aspects of our work, what more specifically are some of the elements of learning and learning environments which impact us? As a starter, response to this question provides a foundation upon which student affairs, no matter how structured, is built.

---

**A number of disciplines and theories may be applied in our work. Our problem is that we think we need a theory of our own.—Smith**

---

*Learning, for our purposes, is defined as changes in behavior as the individual interacts with an ever-expanding environment* (Jones, 1967). New knowledge leapfrogs upon previous knowledge, new ways of organizing material are discovered, and learning is hierarchically structured and ordered. Moreover, for such learning to occur, the student must be actively engaged in the process and must assume final responsibility for his or her development. The changes in behavior of the student are not something achieved by the teacher for the student. In reality, teaching is just one of many factors involved in human learning. Students, therefore, must not be viewed as passive recipients of attitudes, values, and ideas of the teacher but rather as active participants in the learning process.

According to Galileo, "You cannot teach a man anything; you can only help him to find it within himself." Milton also provided important understanding of the role of the student in the learning process: "No one person can learn from another. In the final analysis, learning occurs within the learner, and the responsibility can reside only with him." (As cited in Dutton, 1973). The critical questions for the institution are, What types of experiences are most likely to predispose the individual student to learn, and how should these experiences be packaged and metered for the most effective learning?

A basic assumption is that true learning is a process that engages the total person in the development of diverse competencies. Though the three authors vary in their descriptions, Heath (1968), Chickering (1972), and Perry (1968) have defined critical dimensions of growth and noted the competencies which all persons must develop as they mature. The sharpening of intellectual skills and preprofessional or professional competencies represents the primary goal of the educational enterprise; this rightly has received the greatest attention over the years. Yet, coming to grips with personal strengths and limitations, identity, autonomy, values, feelings, and purpose is also critical in human development. To assume that only cognitive development is involved in the learning process is to fail to recognize that human development cannot be neatly categorized into sets of qualities and capacities like some system of intellectual ZIP codes. The various needs are met together, and growth in one area of competence enhances growth in others.

The institution plays a facilitating role; it delivers a flow of ideas, values, and issues; from such a source students should learn to synthesize and apply knowledge and to relate this knowledge to themselves and their society. To be effective, the focus must be on the individual, not upon the course of study. The learning experiences should be designed to serve the diverse needs, abilities, and learning styles of individuals; to take into account their respective abilities and their readiness to learn at various levels of development and at different rates. Some learn best through reading, writing, and abstract thinking, while others learn through direct application of and involvement in practical experiences.

Turning more to the learning environment itself, the classrooms of our institutions focus upon critical subject matter in an effort to give the student a sound basis for continued exploration. The subject matter is necessarily selective. The ablest teachers also attempt to provide students with tools to continue their education; to know how to unearth facts and test them instead of succumbing to rumor and myth; to know how they can adapt to change as well as to be a participant in discoveries leading to future change. However, individuals must learn to integrate these various segments of knowledge with their own aspirations and desires. Despite its centrality to the development of the learner, the classroom in most cases gives small opportunity to support this concept.

Therefore, the learning experience must encompass the wide range of educational activities, both curricular and extracurricular, that a dynamic and stimulating campus provides. Institutions must be concerned with the development of the formal curriculum and attention must also be directed to the infinite settings outside the classroom which provide the student with opportunities to clarify values and purposes, confront ideas, emotions, and issues, bring new information to bear upon situations or new ways to organize information, accept the consequences of behavior, and grow in ability to lead and relate to others. The most hard-bitten academician will admit, if grudgingly, that learning is not restricted to the classroom and laboratory but may also occur in residence halls, student activities, counseling sessions, and a variety of other settings outside the classroom, where students interact with others and come into contact with ideas, values, and problems. In fact, there are infinite opportunities for learning in the quality academic community (Appleton, 1974).

**We provide the places where learning expands, where the intellectual animal comes alive.—Peters**

It is proper for our institutions of higher education to develop a learning environment which includes the formal curriculum as well as the settings outside the classroom in which the student can clarify values and purposes, confront ideas and issues, experiment, taste, and test, learn to manage emotions, accept the consequences of one's behavior, and grow in ability to relate to others.

Of course, an essential question is, "Can an institution respond to all human developmental needs?" By Galileo's rubric, it can respond to very few: The university or college is only the house in which the person carries on the process of "finding knowledge within himself." But certainly some needs are within the purview of institutional purpose and philosophy; others may be recognized as important but beyond institutional purpose and influence—perhaps left to other institutions of our society to identify and nurture. Which needs will be served and how are questions that each institution must answer for itself.

> **Student development is a new phrase for old behavior.—Rhatigan**

## Student Affairs As a Learning Reinforcement System

Student affairs deans contribute to the learning environment through support programs and services which are designed to assist students in clarifying and achieving their educational goals and the institution in maintaining the learning environment conducive to attaining its educational purposes. These programs and services focus upon personal, interpersonal, and physical development, on the one hand, and upon the intellectual needs of students on the other.

Williamson (1961) has described student personnel work in terms of "educative relationships with students":

> In certain instances, these service relationships assume the function of preparation for other types of educative relationships which take place in the classroom, laboratory, and library. In some they are restorative of skills, motivations, and necessary orientation to the classroom type of education. But still other educative relationships occur outside of the formal classroom relationship.

More specifically, student affairs functions can be viewed as a system of learning reinforcement programs and services. The following general groupings of activity serve only to illustrate:

1.  Academic support programs (including admission, registration, counseling, advising, and learning assistance)

2.  Recreation and culture (e.g., athletics, recreation programs, concerts, and lectures)

3.  Financial assistance

4.  Residential and food programs

5.  Career advising, placement, and various counseling support programs

6.  Physical health and safety operations

7.  Services for discrete constituencies (e.g., services to disabled, international, and Third World students)

8.  Student activities and campus governance

9.  Campus conduct administration

10. Research and needs assessment

---

**The question here is not the organization necessary but what functions are needed which the faculty or other administrative units would not pick up.—Manicur**

---

Although structure and content may vary and will change both in emphasis and specifics on each campus and at different times, the activities listed above have been carried on in some form by most institutions. At the present time, in spite of steady-state enrollment and a tight fiscal situation, such activities generally have been retained on most campuses. Throughout, the dean also has often served as the team leader in bringing together the campus entities that deal with campus student needs and values. To be sure, in some institutions program levels have been reduced, functions have been reassigned, and programs have been dropped. Yet, the basic framework and content of the student affairs program remain. That they continue in some form suggests that if specific programs or vital parts of them were dropped, the essential services and activities would reemerge—true, with some change in form and structure but not in essential thrust and substance.

## Role of the Dean in the Learning Process

How should the dean implement this learning reinforcement system? What factors contribute to the dean's effectiveness in the learning process? Although the role is always affected by institutional and personal considerations, its critical components, consistent with the historical and conceptual perspective presented in this book may be described as follows:

1. Participation in the development and refinement of institutional goals, priorities, and policy, and allocation of resources to achieve stated goals.

2. Collaboration with students and faculty colleagues to assess student needs, to meet and to identify barriers to student learning.

3. Participation in the development of the learning environment, including educational programs and support services; integration of concurrent experiences with educational programs to achieve student objectives and needs; administration of essential support services.

4. Assumption of responsibility to maintain a healthy community that is responsive to changing needs and conditions; help insure that students are able to participate in aspects of the setting which affect them.

5. Clarification of rights and responsibilities and, in light of changing needs and conditions, development of a system of governance and order as well as a means to redress grievances.

6. Just plain deaning—being the person to call upon when trouble brews or help is needed.

To contribute in these areas, the dean must be much more than a "manager of services" and a "controller of behavior"; fundamentally, the dean must be a policy strategist, evaluator, change agent, and authority on human development as well as an effective administrator of programs and services. But the dean must also be a mentor, a model upon which others may depend. To perform these functions, the dean must understand and be able to articulate theories of human and community development, to assess and interpret student needs, and to evaluate the effectiveness of programs and services in meeting needs and goals. Effective performance in these areas requires knowledge of the behavioral sciences, research and evaluation theory and methodology, and organizational and management theory. No less important is the development of a style which enables the dean to motivate, challenge, and support.

---

**There is so much good work to be done that it is almost impossible for us to foul it up.—Rhatigan**

---

An important determinant of the effectiveness of the dean and the student affairs staff is how they are perceived and how their role is defined in the academic community. Incorrect perceptions of roles served by other members of the academic community can have an obvious negative impact on the quality of work performed. Perceptions of the role and responsibilities of one such administrator, the "dean of students," was the subject of a NASPA study of 1970 (Dutton, Appleton, Birch). The study, which gathered data from students, deans of students, presidents and faculty, *indicated that the dean's job should be to help students in their development and to serve as an advocate for them.* Students felt that the control aspects of the job should be deemphasized, while presidents attached greater importance to maintaining discipline and upholding standards and values. The study reached the following conclusion: *The data indicated that deans function in the midst of widely conflicting expectations and perhaps provide a basis for understanding why deans experience role ambiguity, confusion, and sometimes conflict with members of the academic community.*

An important question then, is, How can a student affairs dean play a vital role in the learning process in light of his/her conflict in perception of role? First, individual values and convictions must be assessed. What does the administrator believe, what values motivate and guide behavior? Are the person's values and convictions consistent with the institutionally defined role? The administrator must understand institutional purpose, values, and philosophy and ultimately that his or her effectiveness will depend on the compatibility of his or her beliefs, conviction, and behavior with the institutional mission, style, and values. If not, there are clear choices: (1) Modify beliefs and behaviors to conform to the prescribed role; (2) work to change the role to bring it into line with personal values and convictions; or (3) change jobs.

**Would student affairs really be created to foster learning? Only if there are complementary responsibilities which the faculty and administration view as necessary.—Appleton**

But the central factor in determining his or her success is the degree of the dean's commitment to the development of students. Student affairs structures and programs will vary from institution to institution, but what must be held in common is a desire to influence the lives of students by direct contact or indirect assistance through the development of programs, services, and policies or the administration and management of functions that affect growth. This focus has been important in the past; it will no doubt be even more significant in the future as institutions and the society become more and more complex and impersonal and encounter forces that erode the sense of community essential to the welfare of the individual and the corporate body.

*Probably the best hope for coping with these factors is to revitalize the essential foundations of the academic community.* Individuals are born into communities and must rely on them for protection, nurture, and achievement of goals. But communities do not just happen; they are created and reshaped through a complex process of action and reaction as needs and conditions change. In this sense, an effective community is always "emerging" and reaching beyond the present to meet new needs. The challenge faced by most institutions is to revitalize the academic community by maintaining a process of constructive response to new needs. To maintain such a climate requires frequent review of purposes, values, governance, rights, responsibilities, and methods of resolving conflicts and redressing grievances. Openness to evaluation and change can keep the community responsive to individual needs and provide the spark for continued growth.

The student affairs dean can help the institution maintain an academic community that is vital and responsive by knowing what is happening to individuals and working to clarify rights, responsibilities, a system of governance, and the means of resolving conflict. Student affairs deans can be particularly effective in this role if they have knowledge of the total environment, of what is working and what is not, and of the barriers to development as well as growth-producing stimuli. Without such knowledge, the dean's task is even more frustrating, frenetic—and perhaps futile than it should ever be.

## Summary

Philosophical considerations and forces within and outside institutions of higher learning spawned and shaped the student affairs field as a vital and vigorous educative profession. Not only its foundation but also its future rests on the commitment of higher education to contribute to the development of the individual learner beyond the aspects of intellectual competency and professional training. In a time of steady-state enrollment and limited funds, this foundation is the only one that will guarantee a continuing, vital role for the student affairs program.

There must be ongoing efforts to determine how effectively institutional goals are being met and to make necessary changes to keep the learning process vital and responsive. The student affairs dean should be a part of this assessment to enable him or her to modify the role and programmatic content of student affairs as institutional goals and needs change.

---

"Cheshire Puss, would you tell me, please, which way I ought to go from here?"

"That depends a good deal on where you want to get to," said the cat.

"I do not much care where . . . ," said Alice.

"Then it does not matter which way you go," said the cat.

*Alice in Wonderland*

# References

Appleton, J.R. NASPA As Persons—Of Masks and Real People. *NASPA Journal.* 1974, 12, (1), pp.2-8.

Astin, A.W. *Four Critical Years.* San Francisco: Jossey-Bass Inc., Publishers, 1977.

Chickering, A.W. *Education and Identity,* San Francisco: Jossey-Bass Inc., Publishers, 1972.

Cowley, W.H. Some History and a Venture in Prophecy. In E.G. Williamson (Ed.) *Trends in Student Personnel Work.* Minneapolis: The University of Minnesota Press, 1949.

Dutton, T.B., Appleton, J.R., and Birch, E.E. *Assumptions and Beliefs of Selected Members of the Academic Community.* Portland: National Association of Student Personnel Administrators, 1970.

Dutton, T.B. Critical Functions and Behaviors of the Student Affairs Administrators. *Selected Major Speeches and Excerpts from NASPA's 55th Annual Conference.* April, 1973.

Feldman, C.F., and Associates. *The Development of Adaptive Intelligence.* San Francisco: Jossey-Bass Inc., Publishers, 1974.

Heath, D. *Growing Up In college.* San Francisco: Jossey-Bass Inc., 1968.

Jones, J.E. *Learning.* New York: Harcourt, Brace and World, Inc., 1967.

Miller, T.K., and Prince, J.S. *The Future of Student Affairs.* San Francisco: Jossey-Bass Inc., Publishers, 1977.

Milton, O. *Alternatives to the Traditional.* San Francisco: Jossey-Bass Inc., Publishers, 1972

Mueller, K.H. *Student Personnel Work in Higher Education.* Boston: Houghton Mifflin Company, 1961.

Perry, William G. *Forms of Intellectual and Ethical Development in the College Years.* New York: Holt, Rinehart and Winston, Inc., 1968.

Shaffer, R.H. and Martinson, W.D. *Student Personnel Services in Higher Education.* New York: The Center for Applied Research in Education, Inc., 1966.

Williamson, E.G. *Student Personnel Services in Colleges and Universities.* New York: McGraw-Hill Book Company, 1961.

Williamson, E.G. and Biggs, D.A. *Student Personnel Work: A Program of Developmental Relationships.* New York: John Wiley and Sons, Inc., 1975.

Williamson, E.G., Chairman. *The Student Personnel Point of View,* Series VI, *Student Personnel Work,* No. 13. Washington: The American Council on Education, 1949.

Williamson, E.G. *Trends in Student Personnel Work.* Minneapolis: The University of Minnesota Press, 1949.

# Authority: Given, Earned, Presumed, Lost

**A**UTHORITY IS A MERCURIAL ENTITY. John F. Kennedy suggested that as one uses authority, it will erode. As elusive to pin down as it is, however, authority is used all the time, tacitly if not openly. One of our own deans notes that authority is given by virtue of office but it is the last card to be played. As essential as authority is in our society, it can be as destructive or as constructive as any form of energy—a benign or malignant force depending upon wise or wanton use. As a benign force, it carries with it certain restraints: the surveillance of respected peers or reviewing bodies, individual or group ethics, the charter or bylaws of an organization. As a malignant force, the reins are cut away.

Herbert Simon (1947) describes authority as the power to make decisions which guide the actions of another. Webster reinforces this: Authority is the power or right to give commands, enforce obedience, take action, or make final decisions. The superordinate/subordinate relationship implied may be termed delegation; the military might define it as a chain of command, clanging at times. And everyone who has ever worn a uniform—dogfoot or general—knows that the chain sometimes clangs louder and more often than need be.

The social character of authority is seldom articulated or fully understood by the echelons of an institution—by each alone or by several in their relations one to another. A creative tension is thus developed between enforcing institutional policies and the need to let subordinates carry out such policies—sometimes slavishly, sometimes "creatively." Effective administration becomes a fine art as much as a professional responsibility.

Weber (1930) suggests three contributing bases for authority. The first is *tradition*—what has been normally or historically expected. The second, particularly in instances of stress or crisis, is *charismatic authority*, which arises from a belief by the affected group that their leader has divine or at least inspired power. An adoption of this basis may simply be the personality of a person who is seen—especially over a period of time and circumstances—as effective. The third mode is *legal,* based upon supremacy of the law. In each model, the certifying body is a social one.

The exercise of socially conferred authority, however, is a matter of style; indeed, effectiveness depends heavily on style. Authority assertions by the individual are bound tightly to the definition of the situation, its perception by the actors involved, its historical antecedents, and its current urgency for action or resolution. The denial of authority does not mean that it will disappear, but more likely that it will be used surreptitiously or ignorantly. The way to retain it is to keep earning it.

With this potpourri of ideas on authority as a background, what then of the dean and other student affairs administrators? What are their sources of authority? What unique considerations—of setting, of time, of human need—must contribute to our understanding of authority?

## Authority Given

Obviously, some authority comes from the person who hired the dean—usually the president or chancellor, or occasionally an academic officer such as a provost or an executive vice-president. The ultimate authority is usually vested in institutional or state-approved boards of higher education—trustees, regents, counselors. This, then, is *authority given:* a mandate to act in certain situations on behalf of the institution and for the person to whom the dean reports.

---

From whence does your authority derive?—Briggs

From God . . . and I wonder what Mark Smith would say to that?!—Dutton

---

*Because there is no widely accepted role performance for the dean, administrative support is crucial.* The presence of this support and the confidence of the boss, widely understood on the campus, obviates many authority problems.

**I feel that the ideal relationship to the president is epitomized by mutual respect, by shared commitment to the understanding of the institutional mission, by understanding each other's needs, by frequent contact, by clear delegation of authority, by access when necessary, and by support of each other in critical situations.—Dutton**

Yet, one's ability to direct, expect response, and gain results requires considerably more than simply exercising the authority vested in us by a boss or a board. In tracing the source of one's authority, it is a simplification to say that a vice-president of student affairs or a dean is a mere deputy of the president, though this is indeed true. What of the authority derived from the support of students and colleagues within the academic community? What of authority thrust upon a middle administrator by violence, catastrophe, or even absurd demands? What of authority imposed by messes shunned by others?

Authority is enhanced by the cooperative response of colleagues or staff based on respect, not awe. It is increased by the backing of important external constituencies such as alumni, community leaders, and foundation resources. It is comforting to know that overarching support is available in the President's office, because impromptu decisions often preclude consultation. Yet successful administration depends upon *multiple bases of the dean's authority, all necessary to achieve success.*

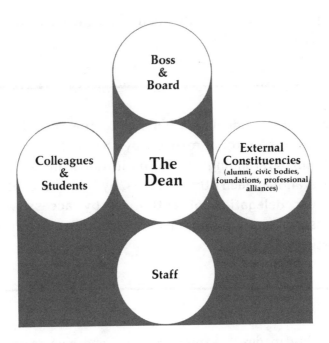

Agreed that authority derives from many sources, interesting questions develop as the concept of authority is examined. Should there be a conscious and deliberate use of the authority delegated by the Office of the President? Should the dean periodically test authority by focusing the restive energies of one of the dean's constitutencies—a demanding student group—to achieve an objective? Or is finesse superior to confrontation? Must one always "win," or can authority be enhanced by "losing"? If tests of authority become necessary, does this indicate a malady, if not a

**If you design a test of your authority, you are going to flunk it.—Blackburn**

**Who has the time or energy?—Dutton**

malignancy, in the hierarchy? These and similar questions require the attention of practicing administrators on every campus.

## Competent Performance—Authority Earned

As described above, authority may be given as a mantle that signals permission to decide and to act. More realistically, however, power stems not so much from authority given as from the dean's quality of performance. Demonstrated competence is the sure way to obtain respect for one's authority: That such respect must be earned is almost the only topic on which our authors are unanimous.

> **My authority derives its power from the legal authority delegated by the Regents, but real power relates to the quality of performance, the quality of my values, the quality of my behavior, and how I treat others and respond to their needs.—Dutton**

Blackburn illustrated this position: "My authority comes partly from the President but largely from the academic community of faculty, students, administrators—the totality of the institution—and their perception of my effectiveness in meeting the needs of that community . . . Being effective includes having integrity, knowing what we value, and revealing it."

> **As far as I am concerned, authority is related to what I have been given, but the power of the position derives completely from the quality of my performance and decisions. I try constantly to broaden limits of authority and establish greater credibility by making right decisions and resolving problems without putting somebody down.—Manicur**

Rhatigan notes that to a great extent authority depends upon a reputation of delivering reasonably close to what was promised. Once having earned a reputation of excellence, of sound judgment, of maturity, of winning battles with minimal costs to others' egos or status, one is free to move without constant questioning of one's authority. One is trusted to exercise good judgment and arrive at sound, responsible decisions.

Of course, it is important to have the support of the President; if other administrators recognize this support, many potential battles are never fought. But successful working relationships with students are an ever richer asset; without such rapport, the dean will have hard sledding, no matter the weather. The support given the dean's programs and purposes by students is perhaps a paramount source of strength. Such support is not obtained by manipulation or contrivance but by competence and sincere purpose.

---

**Often the response of a Board member to a proposal is based directly upon the confidence placed in the administrator, not on the substance of the matter.—Appleton**

---

The work of J. Victor Baldridge (1971) seems to support the insights our authors have gained through experience. In addressing the variety of institutional power bases and their tactical employment, Baldridge cites first *bureaucratic power,* which stems from the formal structure and process of the organization. Items within this category include personnel appointment and removal, budget control, access to hierarchical authority, and control of information. This sounds familiar—what has been earlier described as "authority given." Certainly our deans demonstrate some aspects of bureaucratic power, in that they do control budgets, personnel, and programs and have access to the power hierarchy. In comparison with other divisions of the institution, such as major academic units or business affairs, however, student affairs professionals lack powerful bureaucratic sway.

Baldridge cites *professional resources* as a second power base. This involves the application of expert knowledge or relationships with important constituencies. Though a body of knowledge and a reservoir of skills are required for successful student affairs deaning, the law school dean, the medical school executive, or even articulate and highly visible faculty colleagues often enjoy a professional backing equal to or greater than that of the principal student affairs administrator. The law dean enjoys prestigious professional support from alumni, from the elaborate and extensive legal machinery of the city or state, and from donors zealous and happy to maintain a fine plant and a successful program. The major constituency enjoyed by the student affairs deans, other than student affairs staff themselves, is the students themselves—and this constituency cannot be called upon with regularity, if at all. Influencing students to act on one's behalf is dangerous at best and usually inappropriate; invariably, it is a last resort, a one-time recourse that spends itself and is then an empty shell.

A third power base cited by Baldridge is that of *coercion,* a tactic which may be enjoyed by students or a union or even the faculty on occasion but is to be eschewed by the dean. To sit in or to boycott, to disrupt, or even to openly seek public support is utterly beyond the pale. It may work occasionally, but few deans would see it as an option worthy of consideration. It is an admission of failure. "Come, let us reason together . . ." is the overriding admonition.

---

**We never had important authority. In fact, we became threatening when we presumed to lead.—Smith**

**We have to deal with ambiguities. The classroom teacher can afford to be an egotist . . . for us, humility is called for.—Peters**

---

Baldridge lists as a fourth power base *personal influence resources.* In addition to the values of bureaucratic and professional power, and without benefiting from coercion, the dean will be successful by offering important resources, applying specific expertise, and exercising effective leadership. *Deans of students cannot usually lean upon broad administrative portfolios or a clearly defined professional niche. In a bulky, overextended and complicated bureaucracy, unless they are venturesome, articulate, energetic, and sensitive to student and institutional needs they will not be very valuable.* The price of relative freedom is paid by deans in terms of nontraditional, or to a great degree, nonspecific authority. *Such authority must be won, not granted; earned not inherited;*

*and increasingly sought through respect, not assertion. The surest path to such a condition is through the demonstration of competence.* Influence on campuses depends as much upon personal qualities of leadership and management as it does upon bureaucratic power.

## Authority Presumed

A certain presumption typifies our authors' responses concerning authority. It may best be summarized by one of the authors who states, "Until someone tells me otherwise, it is my intent to move as I see fit. I simply assume that I have the authority. If I do not, I will find out soon enough."

> **From whence comes my authority? I never ask.—Rhatigan**

The following case expands upon this presumptious but altogether "deanly" behavior.

Anytime the institution is involved in a problem, I am going to get involved too. Often the President will ask that I look into a matter, whether or not I am directly responsible. I will definitely intercede whenever I feel that a student is getting a bum shake—wherever this is found. I will also intercede when a student, in my judgment, is acting in a manner which is clearly inappropriate, even though I have no authority. By way of illustration, we had one student on our campus with a severe speech impediment, accompanied by a personal immaturity. He was reasonably bright, not retarded. Another student, for reasons unknown, took an active dislike to this student and was unkind in every respect, from ridicule to low-level harassment. When the troubled student came to see me, he was upset and distressed over his inability to cope with the second student. I called in the second student. With a clear understanding that I had no authority, I said, "What kind of a person is it that would enjoy making life miserable for a person who is already tremendously disadvantaged? What kind of personal pettiness would result in one's getting kicks from stepping on somebody who is already down?" I can report that the offended student said later that the other student's attitude towards him improved considerably. I had no clear authority and probably no obligation, but my own sense of what was right led me to move anyway.

Although acting on behalf of both the institutional hierarchy and the students carries with it a heavy burden of ambiguity, our deans in a way relish this ill-defined scope of responsibility. There are very few who will say, "You do not have that authority!" Once good performance establishes a precedent or demonstrates human and/or professional competence, most people will not raise the challenges which might surface prior to the demonstration of such competence.

Given the parameters restraining and guiding the operations of an institution and the hierarchical arrangements which specify degrees of authority, one always has opportunity to use present circumstances to overcome past limitations. And our deans seem ready to practice this art. The necessity to *assume authority* and take responsibility for actions in any situation seems to our deans to be a responsible use of office.

---

**No one is keeping me from making a contribution to teaching and learning except my own limitations; thus, I am responsible for both what I do and don't do.—Rhatigan**

---

There are constraints upon presumed authority. An institution is not a plaything for personal satisfaction but a living set of relations conceived to meet particular, explicit, community-approved goals. Agreement on such a set of objectives does not mean that they will never be changed, but it is within such agreed-upon aims that the leadership team can maintain current and valid goals and bring them into focus.

### Summary

Authority is *given* to accomplish tasks that vary among various institutions. The dean must not be afraid of power or the influence derived from authority given nor pout about the relative strength of other colleagues. For, authority is also *earned* by competent actions; it may even be *presumed* until someone controverts the presumption; it will be quickly *lost* if not properly used.

Our authors emphasize the importance of power derived by competent performance; they note that the authority to act is not limited to the formal offer of authority from a superior. Colleagues, students, other administrators, and staff for whom the dean is responsible, as well as external constituencies, all contribute to the support necessary for successful deaning. Moreover, personal values and integrity are the mortar that holds these many forces together.

## References

Baldridge, J.V. *Power and Conflict in the University.* New York: John Wiley and Sons, Inc., 1971, p. 171.

Simon, H.A. *Administrative Behavior.* New York: Macmillan, 1957.

Weber, M. *The Protestant Ethic and the Spirit of Capitalism.*Translated by Talcott Parsons. New York: Scribner, 1930.

# Organization and Relationships

**F**ROM THE NUCLEAR FAMILY to the formalized roles of huge bureaucracies, our lives are spent in organizational structures. With so much experience we should be proficient organization members. Not necessarily so.

When Weber first described the bureaucratic structure of organizations, he saw it as a formalization of efforts to promote efficiency and avoid disruption (1930). Roles were specifically noted, superordinate-subordinate relationships declared, and understood staff and line responsibilities differentiated. Yet the realities of organizational life seldom fit the model Weber has drawn; for individual staff members are not prone to remain unchanged during their entire lives. Motives for participation in the organization vary, and individuals typically crave status. Competition for position colors the interpretation of duty; mobility rather than continuity becomes an aspiration.

*Akin to competition for the fewer high-level jobs required by the pyramidal structure of the bureaucracy is the tendency away from communication and cooperation in order to feed personal mobility.* Thus, a requirement for efficient organization may be compromised by the staff person's seeing the present task as an important stepping stone to a more prestigious role in the organization. Counter-forces are at work.

Reinforcing this concept is the need to delegate while still being assured that the assignment will be completed. There is the perpetual tension between discretion given to a staff member and the necessity to complete specific tasks. For instance, respect for a staff member could cause a staff leader not to verbalize his or her expectations, for such "orders" would negate the possibility of creative innovations by the incumbent. Thus, communication can become muted and implicit cues can replace explicit communiques. The milieu thus can become increasingly foggy and ambiguity-ridden.

How do our eight deans respond to organizational issues? This chapter deals with leadership, organization, relations within the student affairs units, and relations with units outside these areas of direct responsibility.

## The Dean As Staff Leader

The principles supporting administrative leadership behavior are not fundamentally different in any institution; consequently there are common characteristics of successful deans regardless of their work setting. These characteristics seem to include sensitivity to the needs of those around them and to the purposes of the institution; personal qualities such as courage, vigor, and creativity; a sound conceptual basis from which to work in planning, making day-to-day decisions, and handling crises; and a recognition or awareness of the personal and institutional values that guide behavior.

> **All institutions call for intelligence, decision-making ability, understanding of human behavior, planning ability, integrity, ability to avoid expediency, and ability to avoid self-serving politics.—Smith**

At the same time, there are differences among institutions, and a range of demands reflecting the unique character of the institution which the successful leader must take into account. In larger institutions, there is inevitably more emphasis upon working through others to accomplish institutional goals. Planning strategies at such institutions may be more complicated and more difficult to implement. In smaller institutions, closer relationships may be developed with a broader range of peers, including teaching faculty. The dean of a small college wears many hats.

> **If working with students directly is an aspiration of a person entering the field, it is likely that the small college or community college setting should be chosen.—Rhatigan**

Not surprisingly, the dean of a small college believes that weaknesses in relating to students or other administrators are more difficult to conceal than does the administrator at a large institution, who views communication as being more difficult because of the complexity of the position.

In private institutions, more attention may be required in representing the institution to outside constituencies, such as alumni and potential donors. This may be balanced in the public institution by the attention paid to governance systems and legislators.

It is likely that the style of supervision varies. In one medium-size campus, the dean emphasized that it is possible to use an informal supervisory approach. Though it is difficult to determine whether this approach is a function of size, type of institution, or the dean's style, the emphasis is upon the value of looking and talking—of simply "getting around." This dean receives written reports, talks with staff at lunch, and encourages a direct and informal repartee in developing judgments about performance.

## PRIME CONSIDERATIONS OF THE DEAN AS STAFF LEADER

A bewildering array of considerations is described by the deans as being of utmost importance in their staff leadership roles. The idealized image of the composite leader is just that: a gathering of optimum qualities and capabilities that could never be embodied in any one of us but ideally would be found in all.

A major consideration is to clarify the mission of the institution and thus to develop an appropriate conceptual base integrating institutional programs for the common good; only then can the role of student affairs be determined in achieving these purposes.

**Unless the organization flows from some central purpose of the campus, the program is going to be in trouble.—Dutton**

Programs for which the dean is responsible must flow from a concern for the welfare and productivity of the institution and from a continuous sounding of the extent to which the objectives of the institution are being accomplished. The staff enjoys discretionary range as long as the creative scope remains within the parameters that assure progress towards the objectives of the college or university. Such contentions may need the challenge of this examination: What are the explicit purposes of the organization and who so declares them? The deans acknowledge that institutional objectives are not always clearly stated. Such conditions increase the complexity of responsibilities because attempts at implementation may veer considerably from assumed objectives.

---

**The needs and best interests of the staff members are important, but only as they enhance the welfare and productivity of the institution.—Smith**

---

Another important consideration involves encouraging staff to dream. The problem is that some people labor to come up with just one dream, and if it does not work out, "By God, I will never dream again!" Then again, dreams can be frightening: They might take us into unknown country where we and our institution are not ready to explore or experiment. An administrator has to give staff some protection against that eventuality, to build in some resilience against frustration or failure.

A great resource for any staff is its built-in competence for research and development. However, prior to most justifiable research, there must be relevant and realistic hypotheses. Fermi's discovery of nuclear fission likely would never have occurred without prior hypothesizing by Einstein and others. There must be time to read, to think, to rid oneself of the pressures of the moment. And how many hours a day can this sort of exercise go on? The paper hurricane, incidental deadlines, recurring minipanics, squeaky wheels—these are but a few of the distractions and obstacles to productive thought that must be overcome before there is any effective leadership on creative problem-solving.

Our days are filled with responses to the initiations or inveighings of others; busyness is viewed as productive; paper shuffling becomes an art form. Reading and use of the library are often overlooked resources of enrichment. If these conditions describe your environment, the chances are that staff leadership is dull, boring, and ineffective.

But the administrator cannot be blamed entirely. Creative ideas and imaginative management are not the monopoly of top executives. They should permeate the staff; they need to be encouraged by the staff leader. Task force approaches utilizing "conceptualizers" and "doers" working together often out-imagine the boss. The increase in staff morale, the confidence emerging from the effort, the enhancement of staff working relationships are spin-off benefits of creative enterprise in student affairs work, as in any other field.

**To pick the most creative time to intervene, the staff leader must be a keen student of the mix of staff interaction, must know what is going on without appearing to look, must be a part of the interpersonal dynamic while appearing to be outside of the creative process.—Clifford**

*The spawning of creativity is aborted if the staff leader is too verbose, too ego-involved, too fearful of losing the reins of leadership. Confidence comes from the talent to orchestrate staff performance, not to suffocate it.* One cue to identifying effective staff leadership is to discover those more competent than the staff leader in several skill areas. To assume that the dean is at once a financial aids expert, medical doctor, student recruiter, researcher, and motivator extraordinaire is ridiculous. Yet many old-style bureaucrats are caught up in such whirlpools of self-deception and self-defeat. *It is a mark of both wisdom and personal security when a dean selects highly qualified colleagues who can challenge the top officer in ideas and effort.* One dean noted the intent to "bring about action programs and services without the focus being on me."

### COPING WITH TURNOVER ON STAFF

The role and style of the dean begins to take shape when describing the response of a number of administration-oriented questions, such as "How do you cope with turnover on your staff?" On the one hand, turnover is viewed as healthy for both the individual and the institution; but inasmuch as considerable investment has been made in the development of staff effectiveness, it is hard to see good staff leave. Turnover should not be considered necessarily as a loss but as a required accommodation.

Moving staff to new responsibiltities, insuring good communication of function, and having able staff working diligently minimizes the negative impact of such change.

Periodic turnover of staff is probably healthy in the long run. Certainly

**There are advantages to a long-term association with an institution. The honest answer is that I like longevity and loyalty.—Rhatigan**

**I like to hire the best staff possible and assume that there will be mobility.—Dutton**

turnover provides the opportunity to review staff productivity and organization, as well as to offer fresh viewpoints and strengths. *But the truth is that we get used to people, learn to trust them, know their work habits and understand their limitations as well as their strengths.*

Manicur notes that, in isolated institutions, as much time may be spent building and training young staff as in developing excellent programs; periodic staff turnover is seen as one symptom of successful leadership, with good, young staff moving to more influential positions. Of course, an exodus as distinguished from periodic turnover may be symptomatic of either no staff leadership or an overall unhappy environment. Sensitive pulse-taking and reading of morale symptoms are needed to determine whether the condition is one of healthy diversity or management malaise.

**In supervising over 250 students in paraprofessional roles, we gain the excitement of contributing to the students' education, the benefit of student perspective, vigor and skill, and the efficient use of limited funds.—Appleton**

Then there is the question, "How will vitality and creativity be maintained in an organization when the steady state precludes mobility?" One answer comes quickly: by reassignment, developing new rewards, reorganization, and control of positions as they become open. Another answer may be to hire fewer entry-level professionals and become more dependent upon paraprofessionals.

TALENTS BEYOND TECHNICAL ABILITY

For young staff considering employment or for the experienced dean seeking to revitalize a program, the authors highlight these desirable

---

**Have they dipped into the educational well deeply enough to be comfortable in an academic environment? I am turned off by pedantic behavior and by persons whose sense of balance is out of line. I like people who seem to be at ease with themselves. Most of all I look for qualities of integrity; with this quality a person never lets me or the institution down.—Rhatigan**

---

characteristics (beyond the technical ability required to perform required tasks): creative intelligence, analytic skills, verbal and written communicative skills, humor and flexibility, integrity, capacity and motivation for growth, a quality educational experience, and educational breadth. The recital of requirements can go on at length: ability to merge talents with other staff and assess the needs and interests of others, evidence of initiative and a high energy level, indication of support for the goals and objectives of the institution, willingness to act in problem-solving, and a disposition suited to bringing students, faculty, and staff together for common purposes in an atmosphere that invokes at least as many laughs as lamentations.

Blackburn notes,

> In looking for staff I am convinced that there is a competence level one must have in administration. Beyond that is the excitement that the person brings to the job, a flair that one has for what is being done, and the love of doing it. I also expect a very strong commitment to the enterprise. I do not expect a person to fall in love with the institution—because *institutions are fickle lovers.* Most of all, I do not want staff to think they have to be loved by students and other staff.

It is emphasized here that technical skills, while necessary, are likely developed on the job. Most of our authors are more interested in generalist orientations; only a few are interested in the technical aspects of training and would eschew "street workers." The need for both orientations may be illustrated by noting that budget preparation is viewed not only as a fiscal challenge but also as a creative program-planning document requiring clear assessment of the environment. This is not the usual technician's perspective or preserve.

---

**You should look for staff who offset weaknesses in your organization or in yourself. It is not a crime to be unable to do things; it is a crime not to find someone who can.—Peters**

---

Integrity is highly respected by the authors. "Truthfulness," "straight talk," "no bluffing" were expressions often heard during the interviews. To illustrate, Mark Smith recalled an incident in which a task force chairman had gathered a working group in an airport hotel room. He was seeking support for a given point of view when a young research assistant stated, "We have done some work to support that notion." After fumbling in his papers to document the tale, the young man next muttered, "I must have left the material in my room." "Let's recess for a minute, young man, so that you can get it." Whether he went to his room or whether he hid in the broom closet for five minutes, upon his return it was certain that he had not yet learned the lesson of integrity when he blurted, "I must have left it at the office." The chair, not being one to be put off easily, carried the bluff to the end when he recommended that time be taken to call the home office. The young assistant was left grasping for straws.

---

**Good, direct, criticism is a sign of loyalty.—Peters**

---

What emerges is the dean's expectation of a strong commitment and loyalty to institutional purposes and an honesty in facing shortcomings and owning up to error; not blind but reasoned loyalty. Loyalty for the dean should also be considered. The deans do not want to hear about problems through a third party. If a problem exists, direct communication is expected—and respected.

CONCEPTS OF DELEGATION

Another way to improve staff effectiveness involves the delicate business of delegation. Each author spoke of this challenge. The message is clear: The delegation of wide-ranging authority, accompanied by careful surveillance of progress, is the preferred mode. The message is: Look for support when needed, then delegate thoroughly by showing trust in able people. Control is exercised more frequently by demonstration of leadership and sharing of options than through role definition or directive, by clarification of objectives and policy before turning staff loose, than by use of power.

---

**If I have to do the work myself, there is no sense in hiring anybody.—Smith**

**I expect staff to keep me informed, I do not like surprises.—Rhatigan**

---

Expectations for achievement are very high, and the demands for excellence are translated in every encounter between dean and staff. It is true that the methods utilized to determine how well the requirements are being met vary from a very formalized cyclical and periodic evaluation system to "I keep my eyes open, and if someone is not performing, it is really no mystery to me."

What is suggested is giving leadership to a staff without commanding it and facilitating team efforts in quiet but effective ways. And it is true that the broader the job definition of a staff member, the wider the discretionary range of action-options the deans allow.

Furthermore, all are aware that delegation is always conditional; should the staff person fail to perform, the staff leader must assume responsibility. The ideal mix may be the admission of final responsibility by the

---

**Delegation is not quite the appropriate term. The staff shares collectively the responsibility and opportunity to make a difference.—Clifford**

---

vice-president or dean but deep reluctance to withdraw responsibility from a staff member until it becomes quite clear that the person cannot execute the program.

The postscript to delegation is to recall that students, too, enter this arena. Intelligent students resent being brusquely told or directed what to do. Treated as intelligent individuals, they can become a major resource in developing needs, assessing alternatives, and assisting in program implementation.

### THORNY PROBLEMS IN BUILDING STAFF MORALE

A potpourri of problems related to building staff morale emerges from our respondents. Developing the following techniques, assessments, and strategies is a challenge to even the best administrator:

1. Determining what is an adequate assessment of subordinate staff performance.

2. Taking the time to give recognition to individual performance.

3. Organizing adequate communication for analysis of problems, planning staff discussion on a regular basis and insuring contacts among staff.

4. Looking for creative alternatives in tension-producing relationships.

5. Getting tough enough and decisive enough in personnel decisions so that staff stand up for their rights.

6. Developing effective ways to share with staff the private and lonely realization that some goals are beyond the individual's or group's current capabilities—or political scope.

Several of these items involve the inescapable responsibility of evaluating performance. To be emphasized is the value of evaluating with criteria selected for review and assessment prior to the event or program, rather than with some hindsight criteria that *anyone* could gin up once the deed is done.

Staff effectiveness calls for skilled and competent leadership. The vice-president or dean is a conductor, not a violinist or a percussion virtuoso (although he may have banged one drum or another for years), nor is he or she implacably the boss. Control is not the game. Rather, our staff leaders enthuse, perceive the long future, challenge the staff to greater productivity, encourage when progress seems to lag. Without playing a note, the conductor uses skill to coordinate the various competencies of the staff upon a single important theme.

One dean speaks of the need for *esprit de corps*, for staff morale, in a manner that suggests the appeal by Shakespeare's Henry V at Agincourt. It may be remembered that the English had only the longbow against the French cavalry. The night before the battle, Henry and his officers became aware of the anxieties and sinking morale of his troops. The next morning he assembled them, having spent most of the night in disguise at their campfires. As Shakespeare portrays it, he answered Westmoreland, who had wished there were ten thousand more Englishmen with them that day,

> No my fair cousin.
> If we are mark'd to die, we are enow
> To do our country loss, and if we live
> The fewer men, the greater share of honor
> God's will! I will pray thee wish not one man more.
> . . . . . . .
> Rather proclaim it, Westmoreland, through my host
> That he which hath no stomach to this fight,
> Let him depart.
> . . .
> But we in it shall be remembered—
> We few, we happy few, we band of brothers,
> For he today that sheds his blood with me
> Shall be my brother. Be he ne'er so vile,
> This day shall gentle his condition.
> And gentlemen in England now abed
> Shall think themselves accurs'd they were not here,
> And hold their manhoods cheap while any speaks
> That fought with us upon Saint Crispin's day.

Few of us have faced an Agincourt with anxious troops. But there were the Berkeleys, the Columbias, the Jackson States, the Kent States. To some in the front lines, the cavalry of dissent in the 60s might have appeared as fearsome as the French cavalry that early morning at Agincourt. And the challenges of consumer student demands, declining markets, the call for retention services, the mixed and strident voices of a heterogeneous student body are still with us.

## Organization

Thus far, attention has been centered on the staff leader functioning within student affairs. A glimpse of the staff relationships with other areas of the college or university and the organization of student affairs is helpful here.

Parenthetically, it may be noted that no detailed prescriptions are given regarding the specific *structure* of student affairs organizations. This is by design: No single scheme of organization is known to be most effective. So long as good management principles are applied, the internal organizational structure may vary considerably as a function of institutional history and mission, strength of personnel, and the political realities of a given environment.

Earlier chapters have attested to the evolution during the past 20 years of large student affairs units—complex bureaucracies in themselves. Some organize a full range of student services based both within and extending well beyond the specific curriculum. Others encompass a selected number of campus programs outside the curriculum. Discussions at professional conferences have revealed a great variety of administrative designs and structures as deans and student affairs administrators exchange notes. Often, it seems, success, prestige, and status are dependent upon the relative size of staff and number of units in one's hip pocket. This is obviously an inadequate and frustrating approach.

The deans have debated such matters as the ideal range of responsibility; institutional relationships outside of student affairs; organizational issues relative to maintaining distinctive student affairs units or being immersed in academic programming; and the way to work effectively with faculty colleagues regardless of specific organization. A brief summary of items upon which agreement is generally accepted may be useful:

1. Some degree of centralization of functions reporting to a president or at times to a chief academic officer is favored.

2. Span of control and the specific organizational structures within student affairs units will vary depending upon local institutional limitations and expectations.

3. Few worthwhile student affairs objectives may be met exclusively within the student affairs organization alone.

4. The need for complementary faculty and academic relationships is imperative.

5. Students offer an important perspective if given access to problem solving and program development.

6. Change in organizational structure may be in the wind, possibly with student affairs being more directly related to the academic hierarchy.

7.  It is necessary to be assertive in relationships with non-student affairs administration and faculty units in order to build important bridges of activity.

8.  Responsibility is accepted not only for managing certain aspects of the college or university, but also for having impact on areas outside the direct control of student affairs which influence the teaching and learning environment.

Increasingly, the question is raised as to whether large centralized student affairs staffs are more desirable or whether integration with academic, business, or related areas is a necessary or desirable trend. While acknowledging that no one model can serve as a prototype for all institutions, centralization of services responsible to an academic leader or, preferably, the president is favored.

**The response must be tailored to the institutional setting; there is no single answer for all institutions.—Clifford**

**We were born as a profession out of the mainstream; perhaps we should stay there.—Rhatigan**

While favoring the more traditional organizational schemes, the authors somewhat surprisingly recognized the value, even desirability in some settings, of extensive integration of services with other administratiave units.

For political reasons, Smith favors separate student personnel organizations. Student interests, needs, and services have never been very high on the management priorities of the colleges, so centralization may "keep the pie from being split in ways that will have a serious negative impact on student satisfaction and interest in the college." Being decentralized may require trade-offs like student programs versus faculty salaries. Clifford prefers centralizing student services such as admissions, student aid, registration, health, and placement, while decentralizing programs for such activities as academic advising in order to impact more directly on the academic environment.

Manicur supports a centralized unit to insure direction at the highest levels. Blackburn leans towards a centralized system and, maybe with tongue-in-cheek, suggests that decentralization may sometimes result from negligence or deficiencies on the part of the dean. Further, he surmises that when the current dean has departed the efforts towards centralization are often rekindled. He has seen some possibility of student affairs becoming a part of a broader university resource model, with services extending from admissions through alumni and development operations.

Dutton is clear in his support of a direct reporting relationship to a president or chancellor for an entire student affairs unit. This design provides the opportunity to articulate crucial needs of the students and the learning environment. Yet, he also favors joint appointments with academic and business affairs, but with program responsibility maintained in the student affairs division.

Rhatigan notes that a recognizable student program with its own staff and its own status among other institutional agencies offers greater opportunity for leadership. He favors a broad portfolio of services—just about everything that does not fall within the normal classroom setting—and careful integration with other units where appropriate.

---

**I guess the ideal portfolio is the one that allows student affairs to make the greatest contribution to the college . . . this year.—Smith**

---

Peters supports centralization, with formal liaison, joint committees, and advisory groups to bridge necessary gaps between turfs of the institution. He favors inclusion of all services, from dealing with the prospective student, through matriculation, to the time when the student ends up supporting the institution following graduation. He speculates that one of the reasons academic units on some campuses develop their own student affairs program is that they do not see the centralized services reinforcing or being responsive to the program objectives of the academic unit. An extension on his campus is the academic unit inside student affairs which has the responsibility for teaching courses certified through the College of Education. These courses emphasize orientation skills, value development, and occupational exploration.

Appleton, too, favors centralization of functions but has taken more steps towards formally linking programs with academic units by acting as project manager for a group of student affairs personnel in academic units

**Unwittingly, we may have been building fences around student affairs by the development of our large organizations. Successful models are available in which student affairs is part of the academic hierarchy.—Appleton**

who are each responsible to their respective academic deans. These staff coordinate admissions processing, "trouble shoot" financial aid problems and, at the graduate and professional level, actually administer aspects of the aid program. These assistant deans also coordinate academic advising and serve as a stimulus to student life and counseling programs within the unit. Thus, not only are certain centralized services managed, but these resources are directly applied through a cadre of persons linked with and integral to the academic administration.

These examples suggest that the student affairs dean must manage effectively whatever aspects of the organization are assigned, but should also serve as a strong voice in effecting improvement in the teaching and learning environment irrespective of the location of given units. One of the authors emphasizes that it is important to recognize that a principal rule in administrative leadership is to expedite the legitimate goals of others. The organization should be tailored to fit the institution, its history, the expectations that characterize it, the personnel, the priorities and the immediate and long-range plans. The structure should be a problem-solving device, tied to functions and purposes.

All agree that the organization of student related programs under the direct control of the student affairs administrator must not reflect a protectionist, "states rights" position of student affairs but should be developed in such a manner as to be of maximum benefit to both the student and the academic program of the college or university.

**Faculty Relationships.**

Student affairs personnel will discover that *working cooperatively with faculty* is the best way to meet student educational needs.

To insure cooperative working relationships with faculty it is important to be committed to the belief that the mission of the institution basically involves teaching, learning, and research, that the faculty represent key resources, and that the classroom, laboratory, and library are at the core of this effort. Communicating this value is easy if it is genuinely believed. Without this essential ingredient, faculty will have little in common with student affairs personnel.

**Basically, we must be able to demonstrate that we have the expertise to support the teaching ability of the faculty.—Dutton**

Further, the jargon of student personnel administration must be avoided at all cost. It is typically pretentious, usually harmful, and seldom precise. Plainspeak is an art all professions and their structures would do well to learn and practice, student affairs no less than the rest. Isn't it true that the current buzz word is often relied upon more than fresh thought and precise expression?

The savvy to seek out faculty colleagues rather than to wait for them to come to the student affairs dean cannot be overemphasized; being knowledgeable and interested in what faculty teach gives them a chance to teach with us. Although this approach can become suspect unless it reflects a sincere interest, the institutional dividends of such effort need not be pointed out.

**How many times have you met with faculty members to determine how you could assist them in working with students, rather than enticing them to participate in your programs?—Appleton**

Helping the faculty to teach more effectively, providing information and advice for them when they work with individual students, and responding to their inquiries will build substantive relationships and recognition of their competency. Patently, good relations evolve from services rendered. "Competency" is the key word in these interfaces.

**Now there is a fly in the ointment: Most of us want faculty to see the importance of what we do, and actually most faculty do not give a hoot.—Rhatigan**

Whether the dean is a scholar or trained in a teaching discipline has likely been given more attention than it deserves. If one is contributing in an area that is respected as a necessary program of the college, then the matter of credentials loses its importance.

Collegial liaison with other non-student affairs administrators is also increasingly important; most substantive student-related matters require articulation with units beyond student affairs.

The new dean who wishes to improve collaborative relations with fellow administrators and faculty has a number of options. Start with an analysis of the existing situation. What relationships exist? What are the needs and desires of your colleagues? How can you assist them in programs which are complementary to your own interests and objectives?

Several bridges are possible: Consult committees which cross functional lines, mingle with student advisory groups, initiate meetings with

**The dean and staff should cultivate personal relationships with faculty. Then it is easier for faculty to accept the professional competency of the administrator. Build trust and confidence by getting involved in the total institution, not just in student services.—Manicur**

colleagues, tap any expertise available in the organization. All attempts to utilize good research or data about students or the environment to assist other administrators and faculty colleagues will benefit the units and strengthen the credibility of and support for student affairs.

## References

Weber, Max. *The Protestant Ethic and the Spirit of Capitalism.* Translated by Talcott Parsons. New York: Scribner, 1930.

———. *The Theory of Social and Economic Organizations.* Translated by A.M. Henderson and Talcott Parsons and edited by Talcott Parsons. Glencoe, Ill: Free Press, and Falcon's Wing Press, 1947.

# Some Plan, Some Play Catch-Up

**I**NSTITUTIONS OF HIGHER EDUCATION are faced with the challenge of developing and maintaining a process through which purposes are clarified and priorities set. This challenge often comes from external agencies, conditions of society, or demands by critical constituencies. For example, federal legislation on athletics, handicapped students, employment practices, student aid programs, or the prospect of a decreasing pool of 12th grade graduates in the years ahead may be cited. To some degree such stimulation is useful, but the unsavory trade-offs may involve the loss of autonomy by the institution and the imposition of cumbersome reporting requirements.

> So many negative comments are directed at planning! One recalls, "The best laid plans of mice and men . . . ," or remembers the stacks of beautiful plans which gather dust in city halls or university offices. Yet, to omit such planning would indeed be foolhardy.—Briggs

Increasingly, the prompting comes from within as campuses strive to maintain or improve the quality of teaching and learning in the face of limited resources. An organized system of planning affecting structures, functions, resources and persons in our institutions is essential if these educational purposes are to be realized and if institutional renewal and vitality are to be achieved.

The daily pressures of our work often weigh against planning; certainly many deans feel that way. One might even offer the view that our "person-oriented" instincts run counter to the different behaviors which planning requires. But where this opinion exists it is obviously short-sighted. It is important to remind ourselves of the essential linkage between effective planning and the various campus programs resulting from it.

---

**Expediency is a hazard.—Smith**

**Planning is necessary in order to avoid disillusionment, dissatisfaction, and fatigue in administration.—Appleton**

---

Certainly most student affairs administrators are planners in a *general sense* of the word. But this is why there had to be a chapter on planning: In thinking about planning, "general sense" is too chancy, offering more promise than product. As a pleasant abstraction, it will impinge only marginally on the reality of our problems and circumstances. "Planning" can apply to the short term or the long term; critical constituencies can affect it, often in incompatible ways; it can be used to enhance or disguise; it is subject to uncontrollable influences which at times would seem to render it useless. Planning can serve superbly in our behalf or as a frustrating reminder of our shortcomings; in the final analysis it can be scuttled by those employed to carry it out who don't or won't. It is the mastic that makes one's efforts coherent and understandable; it is also our best hope of later measuring our successes and failures. It is a continuous process, and in spite of its enormous limitations, it must be approached as a matter of intelligent necessity. It may be more detailed and formalized the more complex the institution. The alternative is drift, or administration by the most willful and powerful.

Until recently, higher education was a burgeoning enterprise after World War II; certainly among "growth industries" it would rank high. Such growth would not have been possible without extensive planning. The period of unrest on campus also required planning, but of a different sort. With the prospects of growth diminishing, the spectre of inflation intruding upon our institutions, the demand for financial "accountability" increasing, the "consumer" mentality gaining momentum, this period requires an even more intense review process.

Certainly it can be emphasized that planning is not an antagonistic concept. When used as a management tool, it can be of valuable assistance in maintaining and/or improving the environments of our campus, and the individual programs for which we have direct responsibility.

---

**Shooting from the hip invariably injures someone else or one's self.—Rhatigan**

---

The process of planning assumes the inevitability of change, and increases our prospects for influencing change. Whitehead (1929) has observed, "The art of progress is to preserve order amid change, and to preserve change amid order." What is needed is directed and deliberate transformation, a modification of behavior that is gradual and connected with previous patterns, rather than drastic forms which may be so violent in effect as to result in dysfunction.

Spoken like a true administrator? Some would say so, and would argue the above position is hopelessly conservative. One needs to look at radical change, however, before concluding that it has long-run effectiveness. During the period of student unrest in France, student leaders were asked about their plans after closing the universities. They had no plan, never intended to have a plan, were interested only in destroying the existing system. On the other hand, some radical changes affecting higher education have been significant, though certainly their enormous consequences were never seen by those who instituted them (e.g. intercollegiate athletics, the elective system of course selection). There are many examples, some of which have revitalized higher education, some of which have not.

Perhaps the appropriate balance is suggested by one of our authors: "The University is one place of social stability where change can be addressed, for it is here that the process of deliberation still has its staunchest defenders and practitioners." Another noted that as long as institutional objectives resist special interests, change is a source of renewal for our society. But to consider renewal in any important way, one must turn again to planning. Ideas are of unequal value; planning should help in the sorting.

There are educational critics who believe that institutions are organized to resist change; that higher education is inherently passive; and that there is ample evidence of territoriality and self-interest at work. Much of this debate tends to center on the value systems held by the debaters. Those who are generally satisfied with the role higher education has played in our society will of course be viewed as conservative in trying to order change in a linear way. If one is satisfied with the status quo, there is nothing wrong in saying "We are going to do next year what we did this year." Those who feel otherwise will attempt to kick over the traces; this has always been so, and one would hope that it will always be so. Our ability to communicate, or our interest in communicating, is a crucial factor in considering change by plan—and, too frequently, efforts at effective communication are the exception rather than the rule (Solo, 1973). Some administrators worship the status quo; others see only change as salvation. When these polarities are found on the same campus, one will never die of boredom. It is important, however, that the idiosyncratic features of an individual campus be acknowledged as planning proceeds. A theoretical process can be described, but it pales before the financial and human issues that are the context for planning on any campus. To believe otherwise is folly.

## Strategies for Change

Creative change is possible even in complex institutions where the immediate and continuing reaction is to stand pat. There are at least two strategies for change: the human relations model and the political model.

The human relations model emphasizes changing attitudes and behaviors to achieve program modifications. Through new insight and knowledge, people come to believe that the proposed change is consistent with their own goals and needs (Baldridge, 1972). This approach has its limitations, since it fails to focus on the relationship between the environment and the social structure of the organization—that is, its values, long-range goals, authority and power structures, decision-making procedures, evaluation networks, and communication channels.

In the political model, decisions are negotiated, and compromises are made among competing groups or power blocs with different values; conflict is healthy and to be expected in this model (Baldridge, 1972). The experienced dean realizes that recent emphases in student affairs in a human relations model sells short the realities of organizational behavior and the need for political skills. It is inevitable that aspects of both emphases are necessary—thus focusing both on the organization or system and its members and their interaction with the environment in which organization objectives are carried out. (Note *power* and *authority* in the Authority chapter of this volume.)

The very nature of a college or university encourages conflict: By definition the academic community is a forum that encourages diversity of purpose and values, provides multiple concepts of authority, and offers a unique power structure within which the ideological jousts are conducted. Groups within the institution are constantly competing with each other for the power and authority to affect, if not direct, the course of the educational enterprise. Clark Kerr (1963) said, "The academic community is like the United Nations with separate territories and cultures, veto powers, and capacity for war. Co-existence is more likely than unity; peace is one priority item; progress another." Strategies to cope with this reality are essential. Effective planning is one such strategy, resulting in information which is one legitimate source of power—authoritative rather than authoritarian.

An extensive body of literature concerning institutional planning and strategies for change has been developed in the past decade. It is not our intention to review the literature but to cite some materials as a starter for the serious reader. *The Planning of Change,* now in its third edition, assembles recent thinking about change processes (Bennis, Benne, and Chin, 1976). Webber's *Management* notes the role planning may have in the administrative scheme (1975). *Planning, Budgeting and Evaluation in Student Affairs: A Manual for Administrators* developed by the Division of Research and Program Development of the National Association of Student Personnel Administrators in 1976 makes specific references to the planning process in Student Affairs (Harpel, 1976). Articles such as "A Shirt-Sleeve Approach to Long Range Planning" in the *Harvard Business Review* are helpful (Linnerman and Kennell, 1977). *Forecasting for Business: Methods and Application* and *Forecasting for Management* highlight the growing awareness of forecasting as a planning tool (Bentar, 1972; Wood and Feldes, 1976).

## The Process of Planning

What is planning? A practicing administrator may find it useful to view it as an active, on-going, often cyclical, and specific way through which institutions and their parts seek (1) to clarify goals, purposes, roles, and priorities in relation to changing conditions and commitments and (2) to establish, maintain, and modify the means for implementing goals and evaluating results.

Planning must be continuous to assure responsiveness to new conditions and anticipate rather than simply react. Since institutional programs are closely interrelated and mutually supported, it should be an integrated process: blending, sorting, winnowing, innovating, and creating what already exists. It is a long-range projection of current perceptions. As such, it has a future orientation.

Planning is difficult, because we tend to be preoccupied with the present. Perhaps this is a criticism that can be justified, a reflection of the heavy daily demands made upon us on our individual campuses. Those administrators with an interest in the future will find substantive writing in our field thin indeed. It seems clear that we are going to have to infer, extrapolate, and otherwise adapt in as clear-headed a way as we can the meaning of a wider spectrum of literature and events that have potential meaning for us. Aristotle once observed that the future is not merely a tomorrow to be anticipated, but has its being fully in the present. The future, then, is always an aspect of today; it is the element of contingency that adheres in every expectation.

The trick, of course, is to understand the interrelatedness of things; the challenge of distinguishing causes from effects, the thought from the event, the trend from the significant, the permanent from the temporary. In planning, it is probably helpful from the outset to admit that intelligent uncertainty is a more promising position than vacillating ignorance. If we expect to have a hand in shaping as well as being shaped by the forces of the future, we have no alternative but to plan intelligently, even though we know this will not be entirely sufficient. We can take some marginal comfort in noting that many writers who berate us for our failure to see and heed the signs write from a retrospective position.

**CLARIFYING DIRECTION**

A primary consideration in planning is the clarification of institutional goals and objectives. In the past we have tended to take an inclusive view—more is better. The questions have begun to change. Should we be engaged in a certain activity at all? How are we different? Are we providing programs better offered by the larger community? Can we afford it?

It is essential, then, that we begin by defining objectives and stating priorities, separating them initially from the techniques of implementation that might be available. Unless we have a clear understanding of *what* needs to be done, techniques are worth little. Defining objectives is a difficult exercise, particularly among larger institutions with many constituencies. Participating in policy discussions is of immense help as student affairs administrators attempt to integrate their programs with the overall mission and objectives of the institution. It is not our responsibility simply to *understand* this direction, but to help influence it. Clearly, nothing is more exciting than planning a program which adds to the quality and vitality of the institution.

---

**Planning is really the revelation of plans which grow out of institutional objectives.—Smith**

---

Programs follow from institutional priorities. This is why it is possible for one to be puzzled about resource allocations; some people enter battle after the war is already over. The annual budget process will rarely yield an extra nickel unless program objectives have already been discussed, are understood, and are an agreed-upon priority, in the places in the institution where this is important. One must typically look at the president's office in this respect. If our requests are only made during the process of budget-building, results will be negligible. Dollars are earned in other settings, at other times. Regrettably no one formula exists—if it did it would certainly be offered to the reader.

DEVELOPING THE PLAN

What would happen if a dean developed a plan based on his or her most faithful ideals? Every experienced administrator knows the answer; such a plan, by itself, is useless. A plan of action must be not only concrete and understandable, stated where possible in quantifiable terms; it must also fit the overall institutional context. Clearly we can influence that context, but once that effort is made and the results evaluated, one must proceed realistically. Spelling out the details aids everyone's understanding of costs, helps focus on our ability to perform, and can be the basis for measuring results later.

A plan must, nevertheless, also be flexible enough to cope with uncertainties. As Clifford notes, "The goal is to plan to anticipate in order to be prepared to deal with the unanticipated." Are there other ways to accomplish our ends? Can we package alternatives realistically?

An important consideration in a plan is its relation to existing programs. Innovation appears to be less threatening if it can be made to fit into the crevices of the existing organization. This may not be a popular view, but it is certainly supportable. It is clear that the viability, if not the acceptability, of a plan rests with the planner's ability to link it with existing structures. Those whose views are important, and who may understand only vaguely the nuances of our work, will be reassured as they recognize the relationship of new proposals with old programs. Innovation has a greater potential for success if presented in this way.

---

**Nobody starts from scratch; each year some revision of existing objectives takes place. Development of goals is, then, a building-block operation.—Rhatigan**

---

Effective planning requires that an attempt be made to anticipate the possible outcomes of a proposed course of action. This anticipation involves exploring options and weighing their potential impact on institutional goals and welfare. Of course, it is very difficult to identify all consequences, and it is important after reasonable deliberation to act in spite of uncertainty. One of our authors described a top administrator as being on a razor's edge at times. Decisions can cost the dean his or her job, but making no decision at all can hurry the exit interview even more. Another author stated, "If you cannot cope with uncertainties, you will not succeed in student personnel administration. You never can anticipate the full consequences of your decisions."

Not to be overlooked in the development of the plan is the quality of the staff involved in the process. If inadequate staff performance is a concern, the best planning will not yield very much that is helpful. Confidence will be lacking in the plan because of lack of confidence in the people. Further, effective planning requires that staff persons with expertise in the areas in question be encouraged (or motivated) to participate creatively. The planning has more impact if all affected personnel end up "owning" at least a piece of the plan.

**Never forget that selection of quality staffs still is the key to planning success.—Peters**

**Implementation of a plan may be in direct proportion to the degree to which the implementor has contributed and now "owns" the plan.—Appleton**

In their book, *Temporary Society,* Bennis and Slater (1968) suggest that one approach to self-renewal is the creation of temporary systems that can be modified or discarded as needs change, rather than slavish adherence to rigid structures. They argue that changing conditions demand adaptive, temporary systems that can be organized in relation to the problem to be solved. This may suggest that on occasion task forces composed of personnel from various units be asked to develop plans for specific programs, recommend new procedures, assemble information, or "troubleshoot" a problem area on behalf of the organization. It seems that this approach has merit as long as there is a permanent system to provide a framework for the temporary system and to permit stated purposes to be achieved.

### EVALUATING THE PROCESS

Evaluation is an essential aspect of planning, in that it provides vital information on the effectiveness of current programs in achieving established goals. This may mean simply establishing checkpoints to permit day-to-day or event-to-event review by staff. But it may involve more formal research efforts. Whether formal or informal, evaluation is a critical component of the process of clarifying goals, adjusting programs, and allocating resources.

At some point there must be a coordinated research effort that is guided by the informational needs of institutional planners. The research program must be responsive to planning requirements, rather than to the personal needs or proclivities of the researchers. The informational needs of the overall campus planning effort also should govern research at the unit level.

---

**Research is obviously very important—particularly demographic data about students. Unfortunately, little attention is paid to this value by most student affairs units.—Appleton**

---

Although in less complex educational settings informal evaluation may produce useful results, generally a formal organized program is desirable. Perhaps the greatest challenge noted by many of our authors is the need to develop better assessment devices. At the same time, various circumstances mitigate, disguise, or dilute our ability to evaluate. Measuring preventive behavior, for example, is almost impossible. Much of what a successful dean accomplishes is prevention of self-defeating student and institutional behavior, but this presents an obvious measurement problem. It also produces some ambiguity and uncertainty about how effective the dean has been. For example, it is difficult to assess the impact of problem prevention—the number of suicides prevented by certain measures or the students retained by good activities. We must simply live with some ambiguity.

The research program can be greatly facilitated if there is a unit or a person responsible for coordinating research activity. This unit should develop research priorities compatible with the planning needs of the institution, design and implement studies to meet these needs, analyze existing data as well as data gathered elsewhere, assist units in designing and implementing studies, and develop information systems that would routinely produce data required by planners. An important function of such a unit would be to report the data gathered in a form that could be understood and easily used by planners and insure that research reports are circulated. Smaller institutions should consider utilizing behavioral and social science faculty, as well as the resources of neighboring institutions and professional organizations.

A systematic means of collecting data from units on the nature and extent of activities and on stated goals and success in achieving goals is important in the evaluation process. Computerized feedback is prized by many organizations. To illustrate, the accumulation of data for and during a NASA mission is mind boggling. The moon landing in 1969 will always stand out as an astonishing achievement, forecast as it was down to the fraction of a second. Without such data, decision makers would be hard put to see the merits of such a program. A standard format for securing such data must be designed to insure that it is received in usable form. This format might require a unit to describe purposes, organizational structure, and the means of assessing performance in relation to stated goals and future plans and needs. To facilitate the reporting of the required data, clear instructions and training sessions for unit personnel involved in the reporting are necessary.

An important part of institutional evaluation is research on student needs, perceptions, behaviors, and characteristics, and the ways these impact on a campus learning environment. For example, such research may take the form of preparing simple questionnaires on a single local topic; assembling demographic information about students who have applied, admitted, and enrolled; or using nationally normed instruments. Many more suggestions offered in a special research issue of the *NASPA Journal* are still current (1971).

Effective evaluation also involves an examination by external sources of how units are managed and organized, how resources are allocated to achieve goals, and whether, in fact, goals are being reached. Usually it is desirable to set up a unit or office that is responsible for this activity for the entire institution and which is directed by administrators concerned with campus planning and administrative effectiveness. When it is agreed that a program requires evaluation, a team is organized to carry out the study. The team reviews all written materials on policy, procedures, and operations; interviews campus administrators, staff in the unit, and users of the unit's services; and observes operations. After these reviews are completed, a draft report is prepared and circulated to all concerned for comment. When the report is in final form, it is presented to the unit and the administration for review and for implementation where appropriate.

To achieve the desired results, external review should be accompanied by an internal review by the unit. These reviews can be difficult, painful, and tension-producing, but if implemented with care and sensitivity, they can provide a foundation for improving the unit's contribution to institutional goals. The reality is that most units will not change without a stimulus, and an organized and carefully structured external review can provide the motivation, direction, and credibility for positive change.

## An Emerging Tool: Forecasting

Forecasting is one of the fiscal management and planning techniques emerging in higher education to meet new conditions. While business and industry have used it for many years, it is not widely used in higher education. Forecasting is simply projecting possible financial futures based on certain assumptions. Those assumptions might include an estimate of growth rate, inflation over time, the rate of growth or decline in enrollment, the rate of growth in tuition and fees, and continuation of certain specific historical trends. Forecasting allows managers or institutions to look ahead in some systematic way.

To be effective, forecasting must highlight problems. It is not a projection of a certain fate. Used properly, it suggests possible futures (with an emphasis on the plural) and not a single possibility. It is limited by the reality that variables exist which cannot be controlled or even understood when the forecast is derived. For example, institutions do not control the legislation of the Congress or states, inflationary or recessionary movements in the economy, or the size of the student pool. To be useful as a tool, forecasting requires multiple scenarios be developed with the keen sense that the future may resemble none of them.

## The Budget As a Planning Tool in a Time of Steady State

Higher education faces the probability of level or declining budgets and enrollments, along with increasing inflation. Institutions cannot allow themselves to stagnate in the face of these realities. To avoid this outcome, a number of strategies should be considered.

Greater attention to a specific budgetary plan will help insure that dollars are thoughtfully allocated in accordance with planning decisions.

Development of such a plan requires that programmatic needs and priorities be stated clearly, that accurate and detailed workload data be secured from operational units, that appropriate interaction between line managers and budget personnel occurs on the development of workload indicators and the identification of budgetary requirements, and that planners at the highest level are able to insure that the use of funds coincides with institutional goals and priorities.

**It is more likely that new program funds will come from old program funds, not new money.—Appleton**

Allocation of resources in line with campus plans can be facilitated by developing the budget in two phases: the *target* or *planning* budget and the *detailed* or *operating* budget. About 24 months before the date of implementation, the target budget should be developed. This budget is based on a clear statement of goals, priorities, and program requirements. Budgetary needs are projected two years ahead to provide a framework for the gradual development, modification, reduction, or termination of programs; the gradual relocation or termination of staff; modification of policies and organizational structures; and development of new funding sources or alternative funding plans. The second phase is implemented a few months prior to the applicable fiscal year and focuses on the specific details of the operating budget. The detailed budget phase is an extension of the target budget and translates the needs and priorities reflected in the target budget into an operational budget. The two-step process then permits the initial clarification of goals, needs, and priorities; the gradual adjustment of programs, structures, and personnel resources in relation to established priorities; and the fine-tuning of programs and the budget just prior to the date the budget is put in force.

Planners must find a mechanism for recovering funds to correct inequities, to implement new programs, or to reallocate funds to expand or strengthen existing, high-priority programs. The development of these mechanisms is necessary because of the prevalence of incremental budgeting—budgeting based on the unwarranted assumption that the base is fixed rather than subject to realistic assessment and possible reduction. Incremental budgeting is workable only when sufficient funds are available to maintain existing programs, to correct inequities, and to start new programs. But in a time of constant or declining resources, this approach is very difficult to justify.

It would seem that neither the Planning Program Budget System (PPBS) nor zero-base budgeting is a realistic option. These budgeting approaches which function as if we start new each year, require extensive time and resources with limited results because it is so difficult "to establish measures of output and relative values needed to employ the techniques as theoretically developed" (Learn, 1976). Moreover, the assumption that one can start from zero each year in programmatic areas is not at all realistic. Many budgeted dollars are invested in people with particular talents, and it is difficult to transfer, retrain, or terminate staff. At best, these procedures might be considered every three or four years.

There are other available means to recover funds to support programmatic changes. One option is to reduce each unit's budget automatically by a set percentage and require line managers to accommodate the reduction prior to the start of the new fiscal year. The pool of funds generated by the reductions would be available for reallocation by senior administrators in relation to high priority goals and programs.

Another method is to have a policy of position control, i.e., when a position becomes available through retirement, resignation, or other means, the position automatically reverts to a higher administrative level. At this level a decision is made whether the position will be restored to the unit, reduced from full to part time, transferred to another unit, or eliminated. This approach recognizes that it is very difficult to modify, transfer, or eliminate positions filled with present staff and that changes will not occur without unusual accompanying circumstances. Most of an institution's operating budget is invested in wages and benefits, and if funds are to be recovered to meet high-priority needs, position control is critical.

Still another way to cope with funding limitations is to determine if program levels can be reduced without significantly altering educational quality. It also is important in student affairs budgeting to ask whether a program is vital to the welfare of the student and the institution and whether the student can obtain the service or product elsewhere in the community. The institution's philosophy must be examined to determine what needs will be addressed and to what extent they can be met.

Patently, an institution must examine itself continually to avoid redundant or overlapping services and programs.

## Summary

In a time of scarce resources and inflation, decisive steps must be taken to clarify goals and to develop mechanisms that insure that funds are used in support of these goals and that careful evaluation is used to measure the effectiveness of efforts toward these goals. Planning of this type will not just happen; it must be made to happen through a rational process and a strong commitment by campus administrators.

---

**Even if you are on the right track, you will get run over if you just sit there.—Will Rogers**

---

The student affairs administrator must play an active role in this process. As noted earlier, planning in student affairs must be rooted in the campus plan. Moreover, planning activity in student affairs can enhance the planning process for the campus by producing vital data on student needs, characteristics, perceptions, and behavior, and on the functioning of the learning environment, e.g., what is facilitating learning and what is not. To obtain such data, a systematic research and assessment program is required, including initiation of studies, the analysis of existing data, and the systematic presentation of data required in the planning process. The student affairs staff has unique access to vital data, but more than access is required. A comprehensive program must be designed to insure that the data are gathered, analyzed and presented in usable, persuasive form.

## References

Bennis, W.G., Benne, K.D., Chin R., and Perey, K.E. *The Planning of Change.* Third Edition. New York: Holt, Rinehart and Winston, 1976.

Bennis, W.G. and Slater, P.E. *The Temporary Society.* New York: Harper and Row, Publishers, 1968.

Bentar, W.I. *Forecasting for Management.* Massachusetts: Addison-Wesley Publishing Co., Inc., 1972.

Harpel, R.L. *Planning, Budgeting, and Evaluation in   Student Affairs Programs: A Manual for Administrators.* Portland: NASPA, 1976.

Kerr, C. *The Uses of the University.* Cambridge, Mass.: Howard University Press, 1963.

Learn, E.W. *Distributing Resources on the Campus.* Unpublished paper presented at the University of California Management Institute. University of California, Irvine, July, 1976.

Linnerman, R.E. and Kennell, J.D. A Shirt-sleeve Approach to Long Range Planning. *Harvard Business Review.* March-April 1977, pp. 141-150.

*NASPA Journal, Special Research Issue,* 9, (4), 1971.

Solo, R.A. Economic Organizations and Social Systems, (cited by D.N. Michael). *On Learning to Plan and Planning to Learn.* San Francisco: Jossey-Bass Publishers, 1973.

Webber, R.A. *Management.* Illinois: Richard D. Irwin, Inc., 1975.

Whitehead, A.N. *Process and Change.* New York: The MacMillan Co., 1929.

Wood, D. and Fildes, R. *Forecasting for Business: Methods and Applications.* London: Longman, 1976.

# There Was Almost No Chapter on Discipline

EVERYTHING ABOUT STUDENT AFFAIRS DEANING naturally points to a chapter on discipline as not only an important but a central element. As Rhatigan stated earlier, the role of the dean historically included the assignment of disciplinary responsibilities to the dean's office: Discipline often dominated the student view of the student dean. The "style" with which discipline was administered became the hallmark of a particular dean.

**Paternalism has gotten a bum rap; the lawyers are now "in."—Rhatigan**

Despite such indicators, the authors first decided against such a chapter, essentially because *the conditions of procedural and substantive due process, and the requirements for carefully articulating rules and regulations, are readily available elsewhere.* Both aspiring deans and experienced administrators have been immersed in the procedures and requirements refined through legal precedents and extensive policy review. And, too, *the disciplinary arena has changed because of changes in the regulations which define misconduct: Fewer policies are unique to the college, and more frequently guidelines now followed bring us closer to the general society.*

Upon reflection, however, the authors realized that a chapter on discipline was warranted for the reasons detailed below.

- **Deans fail to understand the disciplinary situation as a teaching/learning opportunity.**

In a sense, discipline on the college campus is not a "function." Value education responsibilities are thematic throughout the dean's role.

Discipline is simply a special value education opportunity for the student when he or she is most ready to learn—if the dean is ready to teach. Unfortunately, discipline is usually considered only in the context of *mis*conduct, related to established standards rather than reinforcement of a positive action or situation.

- **Too many deans view discipline as "dirty work" which intrudes upon their concept of the dean's position as being a tension/trauma-free relationship with students.**

Curiously, the student view of the dean's responsibilities persists in including discipline and, when that teaching assignment is poorly accomplished, there is at least reduced enthusiasm for use of the other value education resources and program activities of the office.

- **Some deans have come to fear discipline or view it as a noxious and difficult chore to be discarded at the first opportunity.**

That occasion arose with the development of the Joint Statement on the Rights and Freedoms of Students. Some deans leaped with enthusiasm to shift responsibility to the diffuse college "community," rather than to provide leadership and teaching in a new environment that promised for the first time to prevent the dean from becoming a "displaced principal" and discipline from continuing to be free of learning content. Instead of students benefiting from a value education experience in a disciplinary program more appropriate to the college age group, there developed in some settings little or no discipline.

- **To eliminate an emphasis on discipline and therefore value education on the college campus might suggest the demise of the dean and, in the eyes of some, the entire student affairs apparatus of the academic environment.**

The importance of discipline may be illustrated further by the following responses to questions concerning discipline:

"The disciplinary process is but one vehicle of education. It gives the institution the right to say, 'This is what we are all about; this is what we want to have happen to students'."—Blackburn

". . . . . the disciplinary process is too litigious. Now we send the student down the river; we let the courts do the job. The individual's character is never considered, never addressed, just his so-called rights."—Peters

"Discipline is student development. Once this was the essence of education. But we are not talking about that kind of discipline. We seem to be talking only about redeeming wrong behavior."—Rhatigan

"But the disciplinary process is not just a recognition of the failure of other processes; unfortunately, the disciplinary process seems to be defined as the last resort. Passing a law if something is wrong and simply striving to enforce it really is counter to all the good traditions of Western thought, which have stressed moral interactions that would make the law unnecessary. But in the larger society we have thrown up our hands. And what we are doing in education *is like letting the lawyers be our theologians!*"—Blackburn

So how should a chapter on discipline read? It should begin with the multiple premise that the only real discipline is self-discipline; that to achieve the latter requires the development of maturity in the area of values; that such an objective can be attained only as a result of experiences designed to provide value education; that leadership responsibility for providing such growth opportunities is central to the role of the dean; and that the quality of the disciplinary program on a campus is an excellent measure of the dean as educator.

The great majority of students reach the college campus from a home/school environment that has offered only limited freedom and opportunity to develop mature values and, consequently, adequate self-discipline. (This, of course, is not true in the same way for the growing numbers of older and "wordly-wise" students.) But maturity is not limited to any age or period of life. To demonstrate new, more adaptive, or more self-actualizing behavior which also meets the debt the individual owes to others, the growing individual must shed former behavior. As one looks at a decade, say 6 to 16, the observation strikes home, for the individual is now driving a car, not crying for mother's help; entering into complex social relationships positively, if not happily; and no longer cracking brother's head with a Ping-Pong paddle over a heisted ball or Hallowe'en mask.

It is not just being dramatic to say that the very future of society depends upon the extent to which tomorrow's leaders develop mature values and self-discipline, and that these values and aspects of self-discipline can be affected by their college experiences.

The learning, developing individual must depend upon others to escape the now outworn patterns of behavior. The individual often does not know the precise character of appropriate behavior for a specific situation, say, learning to climb a rock. In girding one's courage to attempt the untried, others may take on very significant roles in support of the learner.

The magnificence of the human experience, imbued with courage and a desire to grow, is most poignant in the case of the young person in mid-adolescence who has seen that parents can no longer be counted upon in future growth challenges. Imagine the combination of grief, of fear, of potential disloyalty which such a young person must face without the guidance and assurance of even surrogate parents, nonetheless, when he steps forward to face a newer world! Unquestionably, there is still a role for the student personnel dean in empathizing with students and shoring up, quietly and without fanfare, their experiments with self-development.

The release of the locked-up human potential of every person in every generation is a charge and a challenge to education. The growth of self becomes integrated around belief systems, values revealed in behavior, in intentions, and commitments. Such are the guiding principles of one's lifelong testament of service and dedication. Can anything compare with the dean's opportunity to serve and exemplify in such a setting?

Threaded into the lives of students in residence halls, their use of college health services, their preparation of accurate financial aid applications, their participation in programs developed in the college center, in intramural and intercollegiate athletics, and the classroom are invaluable and numerous opportunities for fundamental value conflict and resolution. The responsibility for leadership in the development of these programs must be accepted readily by the dean; the dean's perception of them as teaching/learning opportunities is the test of whether such programs are "activity" or "education" oriented.

The style and substance of the college's disciplinary practices tell the student whether the dean is "doing the job" and can be relied upon for quality assistance in a time of trouble. Because those occasions provide special value education settings, it is again critical how the dean deals with discipline, or perhaps how the dean is perceived by students as dealing with it.

What are some of the teaching/learning bases that should go into a sound program of discipline designed to promote value education? We would hope, for one, that the "committee" approach to disciplinary decision-making does not compound the problems, but rather extends the resources and the educational impact of the dean's teaching. There is a potential for geometric rather than arithmetic communication with the college community that results from a shift from the earlier one-on-one discipline to committee determination. This is especially true as faculty and students are involved in the process. But it will not happen unless the dean serves as leader and teacher, and the purpose of the discipline is seen as value education. The contention is that human reaction outdoes the law in changing individual behavior, that it is possible to meet all the conditions of procedural and substantive due process while still meeting educational needs of the students.

For another consideration in a sound disciplinary program, when value education is the objective, there is a place for *apparent, but not real, inconsistencies* in the decisions rendered. The requirement of value education extends the "punishment to fit the crime" philosophy to include the "criminal." The process itself may add up to different decisions in response to students involved in the same behavior when differences in educational needs among or between the individuals involved are understood.

The real example that follows may help to show the theory in practice.

The year predates the Joint Statement; the institution has a religious tradition but is free of sectarian control. Gambling in residence halls is prohibited; suspension is the customary institutional response to any violation.

The student is a sophomore, a fraternity man with a C+ average against projected A ability. He is the scion of a wealthy family, in line to inherit a substantial commercial empire. Reported for gambling in a residence hall with some freshmen, he is called before the dean. The freshmen are pledges of the fraternity, invited to play by the sophomore, who serves also as pledge master. They are contrite, concerned about their "error" and their future. Upon recognition of the positive attitudes and the potential for changed behavior, the freshmen are placed on social probation for a semester.

The sophomore, however, is casual about his volation of policy and of his central role in encouraging the freshmen to ignore regulations. Efforts to establish better understanding fail. The decision is to suspend the sophomore for one semester.

A week later the president reports to the dean that the sophomore's uncle, a $125,000 annual contributor, has called to threaten withdrawal of that support unless the student is reinstated. The president and the dean agree that the decision should stand despite the potential reprisal.

Two weeks later the president advises the dean that he has had a second call from the uncle. There had been a family discussion about the withdrawal of support. The student had interrupted the discussion by protesting that the uncle's position was out of line. As quoted by the uncle, the student said that this was the first time in his life that anyone had told him "no" and made it stick; that his father and uncle had "bailed" him out on too many previous occasions; that it was time for him (the student!) to grow up; and that the university should not have to pay for teaching him such a fundamental value.

The uncle tells the dean that the experience has so impressed him that he is doubling his annual gift, not withdrawing it. The real bottom line, however, is the student's return to complete his education as a fraternity leader with a B+ average. Thereafter, he is an articulate advocate of his university's form of "education."

Any experienced dean can offer cases of this type, though most are obviously not so dramatic and some not so positive.

These values can also extend to inadequate behavioral response, not just misconduct. If a tray accidentally drops in a residence dining room and students clap, it is a ripe opportunity to comment to one or two of them, "Maybe you could help him pick it up, rather than mocking him?" How many of us do so? On the Greek Row, discussion with leaders about mutual respect and support must embrace not only what is good about the system but how to expand horizons and correct chronic ills. When completing a reference about a student who is pompous or contemptuous, do we counsel with him or do we let it slide until he really runs into trouble three or ten years from now? We have an unique opportunity to react honestly with students in our institutional actions and attitudes, across a host of issues and dilemmas. How are *we* using that opportunity?

Finally, a disciplinary system conceived soundly and forthrightly as a means of value education should strengthen, not weaken, the dean. Integrated with the other programming efforts of the dean's office, a well-led disciplinary program can round out a balanced approach to deaning and richly complement the total educational program.

In the final analysis a chapter on discipline as an educational opportunity is very necessary. But if value education does not shine through each of our chapters as an essential aspect of the role of the dean, we might as well not have written them either.

# Decisions, Decisions, Decisions

**REFERRED TO AS** the *sine qua non* of administrative behavior is the elusive art called decision-making. Who makes the decision? Are the decision-makers identifiable? Does the decision-maker lean toward certainty or creativity? How are the consequences of a specific decision known? How does one cope with the ambiguity, stress, and apprehension in decision-making?

In general, the elements of the decision-making process seem to be:

- An issue which begs resolution.
- The collection of data, opinions, ideas to address the issue.
- Description of various options and the opportunity to choose the alternatives most likely to bring about resolution.
- A pre-decision, simulated response to the chosen alternative to test and revise the proposal if necessary.
- Staff which can react to and be persuaded that implementation of the action decided upon is sound.
- Post-decision feedback to measure the degree of success in resolving the initial issue.

Reams have been written and case studies by the score have been recorded elaborating upon these steps that make up the basic decision-making process. Emphasis here will be upon selected aspects of this process derived from the experience and observations of our authors.

*The first such consideration is timing.* If a decision is made at an inappropriate time, it may not be accepted at all. If implemented at the right time, it may work very well. It is important to understand the organization, its needs, the different individuals who should be involved, and how decisions should be implemented. Once a controversial decision is made it may even be strategic to consider a tentative delay in the date of implementation in order to assure feedback.

So how does one choose the right time? Some will stress that a certain degree of pragmatism is required. The press may be for "successful" decisions rather than "right" ones. However, one could also assume that a

---

**One of the most important things young administrators must learn is to make critical decisions when the tide is coming in and not when it is low, when the perception enjoyed by the administrator is strong.—Blackburn**

---

"right" decision is merely awaiting birth at an appropriate time! Whatever the case, timing and acceptance of the decision are closely related. A large New York bank refused a loan to a fledging corporation in the early 1900 s. That corporation was General Motors. Some fledglings become expert flyers!

Other decision makers give little heed to likely opposition or a precise timing formula, for they are convinced that their decisions are based upon principle. They reveal combinations of courage, stubbornness, and amazing foresight, or they might just be egocentric, powerful persons. Martin Luther King made a decision to fight racial discrimination. Henry Ford, in his 40s, built cars. Henry Agard Wallace put his convictions on the line to develop hybrid corn, through dozens of generations. We need only be reminded of the discovery of radium by the Curies or penicillin by Fleming, or the marvelous conceptualization of the triple helix in attempting to understand DNA, to understand that challenge and fortuitous circumstance underlie the work of these scientists whose timing was a critical factor, yet who stubbornly maintained their principles.

The magic involves making a decision far enough in advance of the crowd to be insightful or with the crowd so as to be helpful but with some notion that the decision will immediately or eventually gain acceptance. Of major concern is the point that decision-making which is only pragmatic is inadequate. The fundamental bases for the action must form a defensible rationale which is likely to be supported; timing is only part of the strategy required to improve the probability of successful implementation.

*A secondary consideration has to do with the identification of those issues or areas of concern in which decisions are required. If 15 percent of* a freshman class do not register as sophomores the following year, does the institution have a problem? If negative student consumerism is eroding enrollment in arts, letters, and the social sciences, should the institution worry? The cue here is the deviation of existing trends from the institution's basic objectives. As the deviation increases, the worry beads should get more use.

To perceive problems of this order, therefore, the flowery goals of the institution must be reduced to operational realities in order to measure progress against institutional objectives. This exercise is challenging. It requires resourceful analytical and conceptualizing skills, as well as a clear understanding of the institution's mission. It also calls for accurate sensors of opposing, or at least tangential, viewpoints. What are the intentions of the differing voices? Why are they taking this tack? How does one overcome opposing positions? These comprise the sense and sensitivities of administrative decision-making and there is neither text nor tactic that will guarantee successful maneuvering through such straits. Simply being aware that they are not easily navigated is a plus. Experienced administrators will attest to the fact that looking at organization charts will yield little information concerning decision-making sources.

*The third consideration involves anticipating the precise decision/action required to resolve an issue.* Few, if any, seers exist who

> **As a social scientist, I prefer to be like Lerner's liberal: someone with his feet firmly planted in mid-air. In fact, I would be desolate if I could predict consequences accurately. Such a state of affairs would remove creativity, zest, and stimulation from the business of decision-making.—Clifford**

can accurately predict every consequence of a line of action, or even lesser prophets who can suggest alternative solutions, along with probable results and reactions.

So what is to be done? Dutton's helpful suggestion:

I must try to understand the problem and the options available. This requires gathering data either through surveys or through consultation with staff, students, and others. Without taking the time to gather the information and to understand the options available to me, I cannot make good judgments. . . I try to assess the consequences of my actions through data collection, analysis of options in relation to goals, and consultation with those who will be affected by a decision. I also realize that despite creative assessment and evaluation of various options, some decisions will need to be modified after they are made.

Blackburn adds,

You cannot predict all the consequences, but you should try. And you have to accept the blame, even though you might have been conned into taking the wrong option. You must make sure the decision does not endanger the institution. You cannot play safe, however; you have to take chances. You cannot afford to be involved in only a few decisions. One poor decision should not a mess make. If you have a lot of balls in the air and drop one, that is a goof and it should not threaten your ego. In fact, you can take pride in knowing that you have got enough strength to say, "Boy, I blew that one!"

The advice seems to be: Having made a decision by using the best information available, reviewing all the alternatives, then plunging ahead, do not worry that the consequences cannot be predicted with full accuracy. Do not waste time trying to predict the future, try to determine it. As a point of fact, no decision is expected to have all positive effects without any kind of negative consequences.

---

**I only feel negligent if I do not predict something that I believe was capable of predicting if I had been doing my homework.—Smith**

---

The risks in decision-making include the land mines of predisposition and the fortified islands of recalcitrance. Issues are never clearcut, predictable, and simplified, else a file clerk could make the decision. This does not denigrate the file clerk; it simply explains the nature of the issues facing the administrator. The complexity of the challenge attracts our best administrators. Their ability to cope with ambiguity reveals a vital and rare talent.

*The degree to which staff and students are involved in decision-making forms a fourth consideration.* The top administrator is not likely to delegate the process for deciding important issues, especially in those cases enmeshed in ambiguity, complexity and disguise; and the easy decision never surfaces to the top echelons. The staff must be brought in to contribute and deliberate, so that as much data as possible are gathered and

---

**If you cannot cope with the consequences of decision, you will not succeed.—Rhatigan**

---

all appropriate resources are tapped; but then the top administrator must coalesce their contributions into a sound decision. Seldom can the staff isolate all the elements in crucial, top-level decision arenas; this does not put in question their potential ability. The administrator acts at one time like a conductor; another, as a devil's advocate; and still another, as a morale booster. In the long run, the administrator is judged on ability to energize and expand the productivity of staff, to explore and extract their potential for wise counsel and sound ideas. Blackburn suggests that significant persons, especially faculty, be asked not what the institution should do, but what are the options. People are thus involved who influence decisions and their implementation.

The degree to which staff is involved and consensus is sought depends in part upon the importance of the decision. If the decision to be made is to determine the time to hold the next meeting, opinions may be sought, but the effective leader will likely decide the appointed hour, else the group may sit forever debating such minutiae.

*Insuring that a decision is implemented is another formidable administrative responsibility.* Despite computer certitude and long-term association with peers, the chances of a particular decision moving unchanged from conception to effectuation is mighty slim. It is an art more than a

---

**Do not forget that we also bear responsibility for providing students access to the decisions which affect them.—Appleton**

---

skill to facilitate the decision action so that it takes form and flows toward conclusion. This process is akin to shepherding—constant care to reach the objective despite all obstacles, diversions, divisiveness, and strayings. The flock disperses, predators take their toll, the best sheepdog develops a split pad, the weather turns cold too soon—all such vicissitudes must somehow be met—and, to the degree possible, overcome, sidestepped, or just outlived, whether the ultimate objective is wool or sheepskin.

**It is important for those interested in a decision to know ahead of time who makes the decision and at what level the decision is made. This is particularly important when working with students.—Appleton**

Usually, a complex decision process is not consummated immediately by the implementing action. The elapsed time between declaration and realization can stretch to weeks or years. Once a decision is made, the administrator cannot walk away from its consequences. In the interim, the action process must be watched, nurtured, guided, and managed. Assuming delegation of responsibility from the executive operational level, the need to obtain staff solidarity in implementation is crucial. Nor can one assume that a directive will be followed to the letter without specific staff commitment. Acceptance of a staff decision by those it affects should be considered long before that decision is made. There should be no surprises for those affected, because they will be charged with making the decision effective in practice.

*Not to be overlooked are the political realities which impact upon the decision-making process.* It is known that a key problem in decision-making has to do with external persons or constituencies disagreeing with decisions and at times actually working in opposition to the decision. Their objections are usually well-known, calling upon mediator or negotiator skills. Territorial defenses are as common as worms after rain. The collective will of the institution is often obscured by the frequent enveloping fog which infighting creates. What president has not been hobbled by intramural strife? In the long run, top leadership cannot be made vulnerable by continuous scrapping. Few survive it, and no good environment can exist in its continuous presence.

Some conflict of ideas, of intentions is essential to dynamic decision-making; administration-dominated debate paralyzes the idea factory and can open the door to foolish compliance. The in-group can become over-confident and neglect its homework, as it expounds the party line. Conversely, without the discipline of thorough discussion and sound argument, the decision will likely fail even before it emerges. The secret is to avoid off-hand, flippant, or ego-supportive decisions which are seen as personal commands, and infighting which is so patently defensive that it destroys its own contenders.

A climate of trust, genuine hospitality to many opinions, and leadership that is secure but not arrogant are all important resources when decisions must be made. Decision-making is not preparation but action. It is the testing ground for talent, just as the Olympics, the stage, or the podium separate the dilettante from the dedicated. Enlightened decision-making is a democratizing influence in institutional life because valuable contributions are encouraged at all levels. Critical options worked out through staff persistence, creativity, and a touch of adventuresomeness laced with sophistication stimulate the lifestream and nurture the spirit of an institution.

**Hidden agenda will always betray the sponsor and erode his or her credibility.—Peters**

The decision elite earn their status by their pertinent contributions to the growth and development of the institution. Further, in the long run, the institutions that survive today's hurly-burly competition will be those that can attract loyal, critical, innovative participants to the decision-making arena and sustain their interest and energy.

## References

Etzioni, A. *Modern Organizations*. New Jersey: Prentice Hall, Inc., 1964. (Note especially decision-making sections.)

Likert, R. *The Human Organization*. McGraw-Hill Book Company, 1967.

Merton, R. *Social Theory and Social Structure*. Glencoe, Illinois, 1957.

Tannebaum, R. and Schmidt, W.H. How to Choose A Leadership Pattern. *Harvard Business Review*. March-April, 1958.

# Staff Training and Development

"ACCEPTING THE CHALLENGE of insuring that personnel with whom they work on a regular basis are successful in what they do." This thought represents the composite thinking of our authors about personnel management. In accepting such a challenge, they feel professional staff who possess minimum qualifications must be employed, a clear understanding of expectations stated, periodic evaluation conducted, and those who meet stated expectations retained or promoted on a reasonable schedule of both time and compensation. In addition, however, all eight deans affirm that staff training and development is an integral part of their responsibilities. The variable in their approach is the degree to which specific programs are developed for personnel or whether their *management style and regular behavior*—"being a model of deanly activity"—is the primary training vehicle.

For most, specific development programs are considered important, but only as a complement to effective day-by-day activity.

> The best staff development is on the job . . . the rest is frosting. Incrementally increasing responsibility year by year gives the feeling of refreshment. That's development.—Rhatigan

It is clear that the most productive staff development will flow from participation in the demanding realities of the management cycle, from immersing staff in policy matters and problem-solving, from engaging in dialogue with students and faculty, from preparation for speeches and articles, and from offering staff evaluation and assessment. Even the surprises of a normal day or the budgetary process has the potential for promoting growth on the part of staff.

---

**I have never been one to depend too much on staff training. I would rather gather budget heads to hear an exciting development . . . I like to talk with individual staffers about their careers.—Blackburn**

---

The challenge presented by the steady state of enrollment and resources, the necessity to trim programs and to make troublesome decisions—even these difficulties have added to the development of a number of staff. Reducing budgets, moving some staff from 12- to 10-month appointments, and reallocation of staff have been a very difficult but growth-producing opportunity for some.

Good management is at the foundation of good staff development. Some deans note the value of blending "conceptualizers" and "doers," discovering ways to encourage flair and creativity, and delegating sufficient authority. Another comments about rewarding good performance by broadening assignments, moving qualified staff to new positions or unique opportunities, and enabling staff to cross over functional lines to achieve what is important. Participating with staff in planning, insuring that promises are met, and using the "teachable moment" also encourage productivity, morale, and staff integration. *The message is clear: Staff grow and sharpen their techniques by being supported and given real responsibility.*

---

**I expect high performance from day one, so I am not waiting around or engaging in patient growth observation. I support staff, right or wrong, but they had better learn from their mistakes.—Smith**

---

The equation long ago developed by Argyris (1954) and Bakke (1950) is appropriate here. Simply stated, it is the contention that a reciprocal process is continual between the organization and the staff worker. The organization attempts by selection, training, and providing pertinent experience to create a competent deputy of the organization. In return, the person will enhance, develop, and extend the accomplishments of the organization (in this context, a college or university). As a dividend for services, the incumbent improves his or her skills and talents through the experience. Coordinating the growth of staff workers represents a parallel fulfillment of the aspirations of the institution because the person is improving talents in favor of the institution.

---

**Staff Development can grow out of evaluation of personnel.—Dutton**

**I have my staff evaluate me.—Manicur**

**Is that before or after raises go out?—Rhatigan**

---

Thus, staff development is not a frill, an activity tossed into a two-hour session once a month, but an extension of continuous, effective personnel management. Our deans believe they are generating training experiences constantly; their emphasis is on individual modeling. For some, it is even difficult to separate formal development programs from a personal life-style of teaching, of interacting socially with colleagues, or creating excitement among the staff in the context of daily work. To reinforce, to nudge, to dream and think of the total institution—this leadership provides the substance of staff training.

---

**I am older, they're younger, so I run the place like a class—and I do a lot of teaching.—Smith**

---

## Personal Examples of Development

Our deans were asked to reflect upon experiences that came quickly to mind as being most significant in their own development. The aspects of good management already emphasized are well illustrated in these responses. The impact of key models cannot be overemphasized; professional development is not a feature consigned to something that is the equivalent of the classroom. Following are selected examples of these personal experiences noted by Briggs, Dutton, Manicur, and Peters.

## Briggs

In my undergraduate days I was a reader to the Dean of the College while concurrently serving as president of the College Association (the all-college governing body for all nonclassroom activity). Dean Dimock gave me an unusual amount of attention, never telling me precisely what to do but outlining tasks, suggesting options, noting deadlines to respect and common projects in which we shared responsibility.

Inasmuch as he was the architect of the College Association, we would also examine its successes and foibles. I shall never forget one occasion when I had organized a rather complete morning program involving 25 to 30 persons but was invisible in the production: orchestrating the performance, checking on arrangements, etc. The Dean came in just as the performance was about to begin. He leaned down to say that quiet leadership, invisible to most, was his preferred way of doing business. The style of our relationship came close to father-son. He cared. He challenged. He so enjoyed seeing me be productive. A year after graduation he hired me to teach and in 1958 he convinced me to come to San Francisco.

I am not suggesting that "sponsorship" is always tied to growth, but I do believe that staff training is really an educator's job. Conceptualization, orientation to the related issues, staff challenging and sharing, respecting clients and each other—all these are tools in the trainee teacher's kit.

## Dutton

At Oakland in the early 60s we were forced to deal with student behavioral problems that involved the use of obscenities and/or offensive language in the newspaper and in theatrical productions. Our response to these situations was complicated by the fact that campus policy and legal requirements were a little fuzzy and that many students and some faculty seemed to want almost unlimited freedom. It was necessary to try to understand the concerns of the public, the legislature, and trustees, and to develop a course of action that accommodated the diversity of positions, legal realities, and the welfare of the campus community. This involved doing research; having, at times, painful dialogue with students, faculty and others; and developing a course of action which I trust was based on principle. This type of experience was probably more effective in my development than any workshop or conference . . .

Another growth-producing experience occurred at Davis when I dealt with the problem of minority student access to the University. In the early 1970s, we were under considerable pressure to expand the number of minority students, but there were very real barriers to accomplishing this end. For example, there were financial aid barriers; the academic standing policies of the University made it difficult for students admitted to survive; and it was not possible to modify admissions standards. Still, the need existed for improved access and academic support. It was necessary to analyze the problem in the context of campus goals and priorities and then to develop meaningful approaches in the consultation with the various parties involved. This was a demanding and laborious process, but the very nature of the process forced learning that would not have otherwise occurred. In addition, the Chancellor was very willing to allow freedom of action and was most supportive as negotiations were conducted with representatives of ethnic minority groups.

The *Bakke* Case involves one of the critical issues facing higher education and the country, i.e., should preference be given to race in admissions in order to insure racial diversity in the medical profession and to compensate for the effects of pervasive discrimination against minorities? I have provided liaison with our attorneys, the medical school, and minority groups. This has exposed me to critical legal, moral, and policy questions and the intense feelings of the parties involved. I also have had to devise means of keeping the campus community informed about the key issues in the case and the process of review by the courts. The necessity of grappling with key issues, conversing with the parties involved and responding to conflict and stress have contributed to my growth.

## Manicur

As with so many of the other contributors, we went to graduate school when there were very few internship opportunities, other than those staffing roles we served in the residence halls. Some few of us were fortunate to be involved in on-campus practicum experiences. *While these experiences were all very good, the most effective training, for me, was derived from my interaction and personal relationship with the faculty and staff and other professionals I came to know during the process.*

For example, my training began when I was an undergraduate student. For three years I was employed as a student staff member in the Dean of Women's office. My dean was a historian by profession, a former missionary, and a person who placed great value on exploration of nature, appreciation of life, and a commitment to correcting social injustices among people. From my first day on the job, throughout the three years I worked with her, I was impressed with her devotion, leadership, and sensitivity to student concerns. (To digress for a moment, when I entered college, I had no intention of becoming a dean. However, before I left college, my goal had been firmly set.)

Now to analyze. The dean was not trained in student personnel practices. She was a professional, active in the Women's Deans organization, and very strong and forceful in representing student concerns. She was a role model, but she was not aware of her influence on me. Neither was I aware, until much later, of the impression she made on my life. Her teaching was done by example. The learning, I am certain, occurred slowly over the years as I worked with her. Even though I have had years of graduate work and experience since my undergraduate days, my leadership style today is very much the same as that of my undergraduate school Dean of Women.

A second experience which taught me more than I realized at the time I was involved in it occurred while completing my doctorate degree. I chose to be involved in independent study with the person in charge of building residence halls. This person, a woman, happened to be a strong, dynamic, self-taught, businesswoman who knew her way around the financial world as well as in architectural and construction circles. She had earned the respect that she held by her competent performance over a period basically through her own motivation and efforts. Without going into the details of what was taught relating to design, blueprints, planning, financing, etc. (all of which could have been taught in other courses), I was most impressed by the accomplishments this person had achieved through her strong will, determination, resourcefulness, and ability to learn from others. She understood the politics of the business world, and she knew how to get things done. I have often reflected on this experience and found that my time with this person was well-spent. Never did I realize that I would be in a position someday where I would find it necessary to draw strength and encouragement from what I know she achieved.

My own training seems to have been centered around the people I knew or those with whom I worked in "on-the-job" experiences. In reflection, I have taken a little from many people.

In addition, as a person attracted to the practical, I found professional organizations to be useful laboratories for training very early in my career. One's strengths and weaknesses can best be tested by opportunities to perform and be judged by one's peers. We were encouraged by our professional trainers to present programs and speeches in professional meetings. These opportunities seemed to be one way to test the theory we were learning.

I am convinced that the best training for me has been in the opportunities I have been given to perform at a level which has been challenging. Expectations of me, many times, exceeded my confidence level. But the trust and support I received from others reinforced my desire to meet the expectations placed upon me. I realize now that many of my most outstanding achievements have resulted from such opportunities. One of the greatest characteristics that a trainer should possess is the ability to see in others the potential to be developed.

*Peters*

One of the most significant training experiences for me as a dean was a retreat held by the president of our University, to which all deans were invited. It came during the dissent era of the 60s, and we were able to assess each of our positions and responsibilities: what the president expected, meeting the needs of a wide variety of students, the expectations of each dean or vice president as they interacted with each other in carrying out the mission of the university, and other concerns of the kind.

The learning experience was the integration of the academic with the student affairs, the cross fertilization of content, and a fuller appreciation of the fact that the mission of the university is not carried out by student affairs, nor the vice president for student affairs, but by all staff doing their share in the execution of missions as outlined by the president or the leadership of the university.

---

**To a very considerable degree the best and most successful deans . . . are born and not made.—Dean Robert Clothier, 1931**

**I think, while they are born, they can be made better.—Dean Robert Reinow, 1931**

---

The second training experience which comes to mind took place during the same period in which I was required under high stress to deal effectively with both the most liberal faculty and the most conservative faculty, liberal students and conservative students, in resolving major issues of the day. I was able to observe both positive models in some faculty and negatives in others. It enabled an individual to develop a sensitivity to how others may feel if their program is not moving as effectively as desired. The president provided an excellent model by holding to matters of principle. He also taught one thing which I felt was invaluable: He never failed to support his own staff in relations with off-campus constituents. That model greatly assisted those who reported to him in doing the very best job they could.

## How You Have Helped Your Best Deputy to Grow

Perhaps the authors expressed most candidly their opinions about staff development in their response to the question, "Specifically what developmental supports have aided your best deputy to grow to present capacity?" It is not overstated to indicate that the highest priority is given by some to this aspect of their work. Great pride is taken in promoting good, young professionals.

Their own comments are most instructive. "I recognized his program skills early and gave him increasing responsibilities. I have been deliberately supportive of his completing the Ph.D." "My interest in her doing new and exciting things . . ." "The most important motivation has been provided by belief in her ability. This is the most invigorating aspect of training for a younger professional." "Incrementally increasing responsibility year by year has been the key." "Our time socially together has allowed me to be a model, sometimes good and sometimes lousy."

Perhaps what is most interesting is to describe situations in some detail to illustrate this sensitive and challenging responsibility which our deans take very seriously. Dutton, Peters, Smith and Manicur represent our deans.

### Dutton

I can recall a situation where a staff member was confronted with a very complex problem with a student publication. I tried to provide a general framework for a response to the problem and then the staff member was given the responsibility to work out a specific solution with the campus media board and the staff of the student publication. Eventually, a very appropriate solution evolved. The fact that the staff member had been given the authority and the latitude to work through the problem was clearly growth-producing.

I can recall countless other situations where staff members were given the authority to deal with complex problems within the framework of campus policy and/or legal or quasilegal constraints, and the fact that the person was given the opportunity to struggle with the problem, to clarify assumptions and principles and to establish working relationships, produced considerable growth. The important behavior on my part was to provide a framework, so that the person would not wander aimlessly and blindly, to be available to help when necessary and to show trust and confidence.

### Peters

I have felt that the experience where I may have contributed the most to others was through the National Association of Student Personnel Administrators. This was particularly the case at a conference where I was asked to present my assessment of opportunities, advantages and disadvantages of a long-time tenure at the same institution, to philosophize, to say why I believe what I believe, to put into perspective my own actions as they relate to my own goals and/or accomplishments.

## Smith

My staff tells me that the most significant staff development experience in the past couple of years is working to develop pride in a good operation and having fun while it happens. More specifically, establishing an environment in which administrative superiors believe in the people that they supervise is the most motivating and absolutely invigorating thing that a young person can have. "Respect" is the key word.

## Manicur

My own past experiences influence me in my work with staff. One such example is in the value that I place on professional development through participation in professional organizations. Therefore, I am committed to encouraging and supporting staff learning experiences through such involvement. Staff meetings are used to discuss areas of concern we may wish to explore in depth during a conference; for example, "What is happening in the area of health delivery systems on campuses?" We plan to cover as many meetings as possible. When we get back to the campus, we contribute what we have learned in presentations involving other staff.

An on-campus experience which provided a long-range training experience for us occurred five years ago, when we moved to establish a process of developing our goals and objectives. This experience occurred over a period of a year with all staff participating. We determined at the outset to learn as much as we could about the process. In the first phase, we were able to send two staff members to a Management by Objectives Workshop where an entire week was spent learning the skill necessary. In addition, we purchased and distributed articles and handbooks on the subject and several sessions were held to discuss procedures, philosophy, and methods. After several weeks of intense study, we felt we were ready to begin the process of application. We designed work sheets, established guidelines, and completed our work in a workshop setting with the entire staff involved. The process was difficult, but the experience was invaluable.

Following this experience, we invited a consultant to the campus to review our work with us. We felt we would learn more from the experience if we had gone through the process prior to the consultant's involvement. For us, this process worked well. It helped the staff to have a greater appreciation of each other. We learned to be idealistic in our expectations. Furthermore, we have developed a better sensitivity for the financial limitations in implementing idealistic goals.

This example illustrates again that staff members need the encouragement to initiate, explore, and be creative. If one operates within boundaries of fear and mistrust, one will not receive the best performance from a staff. Therefore, it is my goal to give staff the freedom to perform and the expressed or implied confidence in their potential or competence. If performance does not occur, it is also my responsibility to find out why and to offer assistance.

## The Planned Program

With the emphasis fully established that staff training and development is not just a "canned program," the supplemental role of specific staff development programs comes into focus. Such programs may have as their objectives:

1.  Improving communication at all levels, so that a general knowledge and perspective of student affairs and the university or college may be developed.

2.  Providing in-service opportunities for all staff, so that they may improve and upgrade work skills.

3.  Providing continuing education opportunities in order to encourage professional advancement and personal growth.

**Implicit in this commitment by the dean to staff training is a reciprocal and sincere commitment from personnel in the division to insure active participation.—Appleton**

Any comprehensive program should be planned by representative members of the student affairs units at all levels of professional activity, from secretary to department head. Limited funds and released time from the work schedule should be made available to fulfill training requirements. Secretaries and clerks, most of whom meet the public more than many other staff, should be included. The individual differences which result from previous experience, job location, and status must be taken into consideration.

The aspects of a training program which directly affect students deserve some comment. First, involving students as both observers and participants in staff development programs brings *a sense of realism to lofty ideals.* Second, many institutions use student paraprofessionals in residence halls, tutorial and orientation programs, learning skills and placement centers, and as health advocates and activity advisors. It is

**Retreats for department heads have been very productive.—Peters**

**A working retreat on a specific problem or issue is acceptable, but my experience with two days in the wilderness has been really lousy.—Rhatigan**

obvious that, as with full-time staff, the success of these programs is dependent not only upon good selection and supervision, but also upon excellent training. Parenthetically, the byproduct of paraprofessional programs is the opportunity to contribute directly to the education of these students serving as paraprofessionals.

**The student body president is a participant in our management group meetings. Other students are invited from time to time.—Appleton**

At one of our institutions, a comprehensive training document has been developed and implemented by a representative group of staff members. A summary of the plans and activities envisioned as being important and necessary for a successful program at this institution is included to illustrate one approach. This program does not preclude introducing new ideas for program activities during any period of implementation. As a matter of fact, the staff members are constantly encouraged to generate and develop fresh ideas. In this case, a large institution is involved, but the practice obviously is not bound by size.

COMMUNICATION

A number of ideas are recommended for the purpose of promoting and improving communication in the division. The vice president for student affairs conducts a monthly divisional meeting with all staff personnel, meets weekly with the management staff in the division, and attends a staff session of each department in the division of student affairs during each semester. Individual departments are encouraged to develop specific staff meetings for the purpose of disseminating information. An orientation program is provided for all new employees in the division, and social activities on a divisional basis are encouraged. A current directory of the division of student affairs is distributed and a bimonthly newsletter is planned.

### IN-SERVICE TRAINING—CLERICAL

Programs for clerical and support personnel are extremely important. Some are coordinated by the student affairs division, others are handled for the division by the university personnel office. Periodic skill training experiences (rather than instruction and discussion of policy) are offered to include typing, dictaphone instruction, letter writing, secretarial filing and telephone training. Annual review sessions are planned to insure adequate understanding of procedures and standards for completing forms, for maintaining accounting procedures and for handling office machines. Bimonthly meetings for the secretaries in the division enable them to be acquainted with the person whose voice is heard on the other end of a telephone line and to generate mutual support. This occasionally leads to

---

**Don't forget the people who meet the public. Our secretaries handle very awkward situations with real elegance; they are better than some of the so-called top brass.—Rhatigan**

---

office visitations arranged and planned by the main secretary of each office. Communication training is conducted with specific attention to interpersonal communication, office referrals, and the "diagnostic" techniques helpful to secretaries and clerical personel who have a high degree of public contact. It is hoped that training will soon be available on basic principles of supervision, with emphasis on the supervision of students and paraprofessionals.

### IN-SERVICE TRAINING—NON-CLERICAL/MANAGEMENT

As with the clerical programs, both division and campus resources are utilized. Management development seminars on a variety of topics are organized regularly, with both division personnel and consultants serving as instructors. Suggested topics include management planning;

> **Once areas are identified which require more understanding, a staff member might be assigned to research and prepare informational programs for staff. We try to anticipate new areas which may require later decisions.—Manicur**

supervision and performance evaluation of employees; principles of budget planning and implementation; management strategies and techniques for program development and evaluation; and skill training in interpersonal communication, in making office referrals, and in the art of consultation.

Information seminars are considered on specific matters, such as the implications of an affirmative action program; training in admissions, student financial aid and records; methods for working effectively with student leaders to insure student impact on the institution. Attention is given to introducing new appointees to university positions, e.g., the student president, faculty senate leaders, and academic deans to key student affairs personnel.

CONTINUING EDUCATION

Though it may be inevitable that attention will be focused on the elements thus far described in this sample program, a number of continuing education opportunities are also included. Lectures and seminars are given by division personnel on such topics as professional trends and the effect of ethnicity on relations, strategies, and techniques for program development. Continued professional and personal development is encouraged through college degree and certification programs, extension and non-degree programs, conferences, and other professional activities. Institutional funds, at least on a matching basis, are available for selected programs.

## A Comment on Graduate Training Programs

For most of our authors, the specific graduate training program in student personnel work serves as only one source when considering new staff. For others, the professional training option in student personnel administration is preferred, especially for entry-level staff. Certainly the young professional ought to have some understanding of the practices in higher education, but the depth gained through disciplinary study seems on a level with a range of life experiences in any ranking of criteria for selection. It is useful to learn about organizational behavior, budgeting, and other specific techniques. The need to increase collegial relations with faculty has quickened interest in faculty themselves who also possess a sound understanding of the educational process. But a broadly educated, conceptually sound person—one who feels at ease within the academic community—is prized by our authors.

**Five or six years ago, I would have used staff trained in higher education programs almost exclusively. Today I do not identify closely with a particular program.—Peters**

One dean offered a more extensive comment regarding what is needed in a graduate program. In so doing, the elements of a good professional training program and alternative disciplinary approaches are suggested:

I would like the student affairs administrator to understand concepts of learning, human development, organizational and administrative behavior, the nature of higher education, and methods of evaluation and analysis. To facilitate this understanding, it would be desirable to find persons with extensive work in the behavioral sciences. I would like to see students take appropriate courses in such departments as psychology, anthropology, economics, sociology, business administration, and management. In addition, they should have courses on curriculum, organization and administration of higher education, educational philosophy, the student in higher education, and research and evaluation. Finally, I would arrange for students to have excellent practicum experiences; that is, opportunities to apply what they have learned in the classroom to real-life work experiences in student affairs and/or general campus administration.

You will note that what I have suggested is *not* a program in student personnel administration but rather the administration of higher education. This approach would give students wider perspective and increase their ability to compete for entry level jobs and higher level positions as well. It is critical that students not be narrowly prepared in student personnel administration.

Whatever graduate program is pursued, the authors seem to view it as basic training, along with learning how to succeed in the job. As in music and drawing, the theory may be necessary, but then the style and the flair involves violating some rules and becoming free to act. Someone has wisely observed, "Get to know the rules well, so that you can violate them intelligently."

## References

Argyris, C. The Fusion of an Individual with an Organization. *American Sociological Review.* 1954, 28, 1-7.

Bakke, E.W. *Bonds of Organization.* New York: Harper, 1950.

# Kisses of Death

SUCCESS AND EFFECTIVENESS in student personnel administration are elusive concepts, often measured or claimed in terms only indirectly related to, if not far removed from, the responsibilities, standards, and principles of the profession.

In the absence of any other generally recognized criteria, the hallmarks of success and effectiveness in this field are likely to be titles, salary, popularity with students and/or colleagues, security (or survival) in a position, employability, reputation (often based on style), positive self-evaluation, and major offices in professional associations. Contributing to the confusion over criteria is the fact that success and effectiveness, not to mention failure and ineffectiveness, are at times not at all the same thing.

Failure and ineffectiveness are perhaps more easily measured, but just as difficult to understand or explain. In failure, as in success, unpredictable or uncontrollable circumstances can be dominant factors. It is true, however, that many individuals do fail, or at least fail to succeed, because of characteristics, tendencies, attitudes, consistent errors of commission or omission, or weaknesses which might have been overcome or reduced with more insight or knowledge of consequences.

Thus, while it would be foolish to pretend that there are personal, professional, or administrative weaknesses that consistently foil success, it would make even less sense not to offer any advice or caution to colleagues or to individuals heading into a field fraught with peril, whether of one's own or others' making. So it is that we list below some "kisses of death" offered with the conviction that, in this ominous recital, the perspiring as well as the aspiring may find some useful advice, some facets of performance or non-performance to bear in mind.

In emphasizing that all of this is more suggestive than instructive, we do not imply that it is whimsical or carelessly conceived. Each characteristic, tendency, or condition described has been chosen with some thought and with the sincere intention of avoiding the biases of particular styles or administrative settings. Each represents something that many experienced, dedicated administrators try quite deliberately to avoid. Some will quickly notice a great amount of overlap but will just as quickly realize how significant the overlap is—that we are dealing with symptoms or signs of a few very basic weaknesses or attitudes that surface in an infinite variety of problems. For what they are worth, these are the "kisses of death", or, as one person has labeled them, "the termites of termination."

1. **Ducking.** The rationalized, disguised, or blatant avoidance of difficult or hazardous decisions; reluctance or unwillingness to take responsibility for actions, reactions, or decisions that are right, demanded by principle or policy, or imperative, but which are likely to be unpopular, or at least controversial or which affect others negatively; refusal to hurt in the interest of the institution, standards, or the welfare of others, including those who would be hurt; self-serving or habitual indecisiveness.

   *Variations:* Expedient or self-serving humility; unproductive or unprincipled stalling (buying time without knowing how to spend it); inability to say no or to say no without weaseling qualifications or weak apologies; directly or indirectly blaming unpopular decisions on others; abdicating as an agent of behavioral consequences; playing-it-safe; intentionally or consistently leaving the "dirty work" for others.

2. **Being A Load.** The tendency to be a downer—a problem-sounder rather than a solution-finder. Unproductively or destructively pessimistic; whining or boring preoccupation with negative aspects or possibilities; gloominess; chronic retrenchment-thinking.

   *Variations:* Self-righteous or self-serving martyrdom; individual or administrative self-pity; specializing in, listening for, hearing, or communicating bad news, criticism, or unpleasant information; constantly complaining or reinforcing complaints of others; boring colleagues or others with analyses of inequities, risks, or unsolvable problems or barriers; second-guessing in failure situations; overly concerned with placing blame; management by objection; seeking sympathy.

3. **Bad Judgment.** Consistently making decisions or taking actions which cause problems or fail to solve them; tendency to guess badly or prematurely in order to seem quick; tendency to overestimate or overstate; failure to benefit from experience; lack of insight concerning one's own limitations; lack of discernment; failure to realistically consider consequences or effects; ignoring or not collecting significant data; allowing crises to develop.

*Variations:* Poor timing; impetuousness; failure to do homework; lack of intelligence or perceptiveness; not considering or caring about outcomes or consequences; carelessness; getting involved in irresolvable conflicts; inability or unwillingness to see problems, issues, or factors clearly; tendency to engage in cosmetic programming or symptomatic treatment, confusing cause and effect.

4. **Under-Consultation.** Underestimating the value and importance of consultation as a source of information, ideas, relationships, and support; avoiding consultation as weakness or dependency; tendency to ask the wrong people or the wrong questions; treating consultation as a formality or political game; ignoring or not applying results; missing the alternatives and qualifications that only consultation could suggest.

*Variations:* Lack of insight concerning own limitations; not listening, relating, or watching; excluding others (especially students, faculty, and colleagues) from decision-making in order not to have to share credit or responsibility.

5. **Self-Promotion.** Preoccupation with popularity, status, support, or power; seeming to be overly interested in looking good, right, or bright; managing behavior to create favorable or desired impressions or opinions of oneself among students, colleagues, subordinates, or superiors; hunger for appreciation or credit; claiming credit; trying to impress the top, trying to impress the bottom; awkwardly ambitious; using present position as stepping stone.

*Variations:* Creating elite in-groups; playing favorites; currying favor; not sharing credit with or giving credit to subordinates; using jargon or pedantry to impress; vanity; self-serving politics; trying to appear intellectual or striving for intellectual acceptability; preoccupation with title or salary; uncritical acceptance of supportive opinions; jealousy.

6. **Lack of Warmth.** Inability or disinclination to express concern, understanding, or closeness; unfriendliness; lack of humor or sense of the absurd; inability or unwillingness to relax or have fun; underestimation of or difficulty with social skills and relationships; lack of ability to maintain good disposition or to express sensitivity, caring, and good will, especially in adversary situations or relationships; inability to say no in ways that indicate respect or thoughtfulness; inability to effectively reinforce.

   *Variations:* Impatience with others; avoiding or responding badly or awkwardly to personal problems of others or to counseling situations; defensiveness; taking self or issues too seriously; self-righteousness; condescension; misuse or overuse of sarcasm; preoccupation with authority, or seeming to be tough; trying too hard to seem poised or professional or trying in ways that constitute arrogance, rigidity, or negativism; superficiality; overuse of memos and underuse of personal contact.

7. **Lack of Humanity.** Intolerance of or lack of respect for human differences; racism; sexism; antisemitism; snobbery; using people; condoning or tolerating bigotry or cruelty; putting people down or engaging in denigrating or insulting personal politics; bullying; exclusiveness; sense of superiority; insensitivity to feelings or values of others; treating people as category members or things rather than as persons; facultyism, studentism, staffism; exploitation.

   *Variations:* Perceiving certain others as too limited to be treated with respect or reason; lack of respect for privacy, elements of due process, and the human rights of others; narrow-mindedness; moralistic rejection or condemnation.

8. **Poor Excuses.** Failure to realize that alibis or rationalizations do not offset errors of commission or omission, unless clearly stemming from unforeseeable circumstances or perceived by those affected as honest errors of judgment unrelated to negligence or self-indulgence; perceiving personal problems as extenuating circumstances and allowing them to interfere with effectiveness; not sensing when silence or simply admitting error and moving on is the wisest behavior; offering reasons or explanations for poor results which are or appear to be weak, insufficient, self-serving, or deceitful.

*Variations:* Blaming subordinates, superiors, or others; unwillingness to admit errors; self-serving use of apology; condemning the response instead of correcting the cause.

9. **Procrastination.** Putting things off, especially unpleasant tasks, until later or immediately prior to deadline; self-deceptively counting on having or finding free time that never arrives; wasting time in the present; relying on time rather than action as the healer; operating on demand only.

*Variations:* Underestimating the importance of doing things sooner and better than requested; not being prepared for requests prior to original deadline; allowing tasks to accumulate to the point that expedient or drastic treatment is required; sequential approach to responsibilities; counting on being able to stall, bluff, or offer convincing excuses for non-performance; creating devices for diluting feelings of guilt.

10. **Over-Trusting Memory.** Tendency to overestimate ability to recall information, requests, commitments, or ideas; underestimating the importance of accurate recall, as accurate as that of other persons most interested or affected, or remembering names and statements; not given to taking notes or getting things in writing.

*Variations:* Placing too much trust in memories of others; not remembering that you forgot; unintentional or forgetful inconsistency or hypocrisy; speaking in disappearing ink; not returning calls; underestimating the value of documentation.

11. **Petulance.** Inability to control temper or avoid hostility in adversary situations, to handle harassing or provoking people, or to disagree or argue without insulting or putting people down; tendency to become petty or personal in controversy; unable to respond fairly to unfair treatment; being too thin-skinned.

*Variations:* Inability or unwillingness to apologize; inability to accept or benefit from criticism; defensiveness; harboring grudges or letting professional disagreements disturb social relationships or vice versa; inability to let lying dogs sleep; not realizing one could be wrong, or another right, or both wrong, or both right; perceiving adversaries as stubborn, evil, uncooperative, or unintelligent;

being too easily offended by or overreacting to faculty attitudes; inclined to create unnecessary or unaffordable enemies; letting hostility or irrationality cause one to lose arguments; impatience; insisting on unambiguous treatment of ambiguous situations; overgeneralizing adversary relationships, assuming adversary on one issue will be adversary on others.

12. **Under- and Overdelegation.** Inability, unwillingness, or failure to delegate responsibility in order to free self for more productive expenditure of time or in order to give subordinates experience; not trusting others enough to delegate effectively; given to excessive monitoring; delegating expediently or to get out of things; not doing enough of own homework to keep in touch with important data, events, circumstances.

*Variations:* Unwillingness to have others receive or share credit; compulsiveness about doing things oneself; overestimating available time or energy.

13. **Disloyalty.** Not comprehending or choosing to adhere to the elements of administrative loyalty; not having or comprehending a strong, clear sense of accountability; failing to identify with the institution and its objectives, standards, and administrative structure; underestimating importance of administrative and personal loyalty to superiors, subordinates and/or colleagues; not protecting and supporting the top; going around immediate superior; going around subordinate; allowing personal conflicts to take priority over administrative loyalty or accountability; lacking a sense of commitment; letting own morale affect loyalty and/or commitments.

*Variations:* Failing to defend enterprise and/or to participate in a solid front; extending concept of style beyond limits of loyalty; badmouthing venturesomeness; second-guessing colleagues, subordinates, or superiors; failing to clearly understand accountability structure; tendency to base accountability on personal wishes, friendships, or needs; not understanding centrality of academic programs; inability or unwillingness to support decisions or policies with which one disagrees but which cannot be changed; letting little things creep to the top; confusing obsequiousness with loyalty; demanding obsequiousness rather than objectivity; asking for advice but accepting only support.

14. **Ignorance About Human Behavior.** Not having sufficient experience, knowledge, or insight with regard to human relationships or characteristics to predict reactions or outcomes, to offer productive advice, or to conceptualize human problems or issues; making vulnerable or wrong assumptions about human feelings or perceptions.

    *Variations:* Incompetent counseling; inability to recognize facades; inability to deal effectively with parents, human emergencies, and psychological difficulties. Saying "I understand" when you don't; hyperhumanism; hyperidealism.

15. **Misapplying Useful Strategies.** Borrowing or mimicking administrative forms, devices, or styles without sufficient understanding, insight, or discernment; using such tactics to impress others or cover ignorance; gambling unnecessarily or badly; compulsive checking or preoccupation with trivia.

    *Variations:* Asking questions one does not or should not want to hear the answers to or which raise issues that might distract or diminish; showing off with theory or jargon; making things too complex; playing unproductive politics; pedantry; specializing in long answers to short questions rather than vice versa; practicing law or medicine without a license.

16. **Shortage of Energy.** Limited stamina because of physical factors, enervating outside interests or social patterns or habits of lethargy; not having strength or drive to work hard over long periods of time and still respond to special or emergency situations.

    *Variations:* Cutting corners or skimping to save energy; resenting impositions on free or personal time; needing to be challenged to really put out; viewing student personnel administration as easy, as an escape from hard work; not taking the initiative; operating on demand only.

17. **Professional Dishonesty.** Tendency to violate confidentiality; rumor-mongering; accepting hearsay; talking behind others' backs; prurience; pettiness; jealousy; playing people against each other; playing favorites; self-serving personal politics; lack of respect for truth; failure to appreciate negative consequences of deceit

and lying to cover lies; lack of principles, standards; lying to get out of work; hearing only those opinions one wants to hear; inventing student opinion or drawing it from a biased sample.

*Variations:* Cheating on expense accounts, with or without rationalization; condoning illegal or dishonest behavior; taking cheap shots; expediency; looking for ways out of issues and problems rather than ways into them; self-serving accommodation; saying different things to different people; viewing people as pawns to be manipulated; seeking respect and affection rather than giving and earning them.

18. **Lack of Leadership.** Inability to earn respect, to be persuasive with ease; fear or avoidance of taking the lead, speaking out, taking positions; tendency to be dependent on others, to need prodding or reinforcement; unimpressive or unattractive appearance or style, without compensatory skills or knowledge; lack of personal or professional courage.

*Variation:* Avoidance of responsibility; preference for providing response rather than stimulus; lack of initiative, confidence, management skills, ability to speak, ability to write; passivity; lack of academic or professional credentials or patronage; deficient planning and management skills; disinclination to engage in planning, projecting, managing, programming; failure to recognize one's position or professional worth or expecting others to recognize it; deferring to bullying or disrespectful treatment.

Each reader should have additions and each may have some feelings or opinions as to the causes, sources, and durability of these tendencies. Some will deny the applicability of all of this to certain administrative or institutional settings and will wish to create their own lists. Others will suggest that to live up to this list would require sainthood or even divinity.

Obvious questions are raised here—but certainly not answered—with regard to training, selection, and evaluation. Perhaps most obvious is the suggestion that, in student personnel administration as in perhaps every profession that deals directly with service to human beings, accountability is inescapable, and the individual is measured by the feelings he or she creates in others. Apparent throughout is the need to enjoy the foibles and fancies of people, to admire their strengths, to work with them on weaknesses, to be honest without denigrating; to seek mutual support and concern. Implicit is the need to realize that giving to others both creates and signifies self-respect.

**Some will deny the applicability of all of this to certain administrative or institutional settings and will wish to create their own lists. Others will suggest that to live up to this list would require sainthood or even divinity.**

It is a sad truism that people are too often measured by lowest common denominators or worst performances. It is also true that there is no clearly defined student personnel profession in which one can become ultimately and securely skilled. Thus, it is no wonder that so many student personnel administrators find so little unqualified satisfaction in their work and why so many, even those who manifestly succeed, still progress inexorably toward insecurity.

Perhaps in a profession in which so much is expected from so many different perspectives and so much of what is accomplished is taken for granted or forgotten, neither success nor failure should be taken as seriously as they often are. Service in our profession might best be perceived as a transitory privilege, to be enjoyed and cherished while it lasts. Success or failure, satisfaction or disappointment, are perhaps measured better in personal values and principles than by the ephemeral criteria applied not only by our colleagues and superiors but also, strangely enough, by ourselves.

# Styles of the Dean

**P**ERSONAL STYLE is the professional demeanor by which each of us is known. It denotes how we behave in our work, as distinguished from what we do. It is true, of course, that behavior and results are integrally related, but similar results can be achieved in different ways, one of which is uniquely our own. Style is a crucial ingredient of management, it is evident in every chapter of this volume, and it is so important as to warrant particular treatment in its own chapter.

Style represents a person's avowed beliefs and principles. It also embraces variations of setting, circumstance, and opportunity. If one works in a setting that "cramps your style," or where an artificial style must be affected, the job is going to have unwelcome complications and constraints. It can be influenced by historical period, health, age, sex, ethnicity, or other factors. It may develop pragmatically from what "works"—what behavior has been rewarded in the past. To the outside world it is the "way," not so much the "why," of our behavior that is initially most evident. It is the essentially consistent manner in which the individual carries out responsibility—some sort of composite of mannerisms and individual characteristics.

**The world is full of competent people, but flair, some characteristics of style make a difference beyond the basic competency level, especially in later jobs.—Blackburn**

It is not enough to say that style is a reflection of personality though one cannot really consider one without the other. Adler's view of the "creative self" may be useful in this context. In his later life, Adler came to the view that one fashions his or her own personality:

Heredity only endows him with certain abilities. Environment only gives him certain impressions. These abilities and impressions, and the manner in which he "experiences" them . . . are the bricks which he uses in his own "creative" way in building up his attitude toward life. It is his individual way of using these bricks, or in other words his attitude toward life, which determines this relationship to the outside world (Adler, 1935).

This is a humanistic point of view with which everyone will not agree. It can serve, however, as a basis for our discussion. It is at least an arguable hypothesis that the "way" of building relationships with the outside world often subordinates the "why."

The arts may provide an analogous reference. Van Gogh and Turner both were concerned with the element of light, yet they reflect different styles or approaches. Van Gogh applied paint vigorously; his brush strokes were bold. Turner completed dramatic compositions by use of rather thinly applied paint and contrasting light and dark shapes. One quickly differentiates Brahms and Gershwin, Franck and Prokofiev, Bob Hope and Johnny Carson, Bernstein and Fiedler.

So it is with practicing administrators, for their work is also an art, a mode of orchestrating talent through effective managerial style. Cleland and King (1968) appear to grasp this concept:

While both a technological and a management base are necessary for the manager, they alone will not ensure his success. Whatever academics might like to believe about their ability to teach technological understanding or management skills, these 'teachable' things will not suffice; there is another critical ingredient which can be readily seen through close contact with successful managers of complex systems—personal style.

The manager must accomplish organizational goals by working through others. He obviously has no choice in the matter, since he can almost never achieve these goals by virtue only of his personal efforts. . . . To be effective, the manager must develop a personal style which permits him to translate his formal authority into real authority—the ability to exert influence on the decisions and activities of others.

One must resist the temptation to view style as a kind of superficial, public relations phenomenon. Anyone employing "style" in this way will eventually be brought up short, as authenticity is a critical factor in developing an effective style. If style is relied upon as a substitute for competence, only a pitiful caricature will result. Most notably, the style of the successful dean presents the most authentic extension of individuality and aptitude. Uniqueness is common to each of us: It is the rare combination of one's talents and their use in individual professional settings that determines our uniqueness and our competence, that finally forms our "style." Style, then, becomes the vehicle that converts our competence into performance in our respective organizations.

---

**Some of us are committed to having our style match our beliefs, regardless of the demands or needs of the situation. Others let individual situations shape our style. A choice must be made whether style grows out of situation or belief.—Smith**

**The set of values that I developed in my home and in my church guides my behavior. Particularly, these values influence how I treat people and how I respond to advice from others.—Clifford**

---

We must leave in abeyance any detailed discussion of the "learning" or "teaching" of style for administrators. It can be conceded, perhaps, that it would be difficult to learn a "style" in any direct sense. It is certain, of course, that we have all modeled somewhat on the successful and admired persons in our lives—but we are not they, and we can never be completely like them.

Unfortunately, little or no emphasis is placed on personal style in the teaching and training of administrators. To do it, of course, requires such a personal relationship between teacher and learner that few would have the time or the self-reliance to attempt it. One can speculate that a teacher could, by working with an individual and after carefully analyzing and studying the person's characteristics and mannerisms, encourage him or her to expand and develop further certain mannerisms or characteristics to which people are apt to respond favorably.

In any case, "The existence of a unique personal style is an obvious trait of virtually every successful manager. . . . The aspirant should recognize that there are few colorless managers at the top of any kind of modern organization." (Cleland and King, 1968) Each person who aspires to a position of leadership should be ultrasensitive to the importance of personal style. The aspirant should attempt to identify his or her self-perceived style and periodically weigh this coloring against feedback of others' perception of the aspirants.

## A Collage of Styles

If style springs from the individual and is, to a large extent, developed "on the job," then it may be helpful to observe more closely the personal styles of selected deans—in this instance, the authors. Are there cues to follow? What is unique in each one? Though diversity abounds, are there common characteristics that appear?

A hint of the personal styles of the eight deans, diverse yet with similarities, was noted in the introductory chapter. Smith and Peters are miles apart in their organizational styles, as are Dutton and Rhatigan, Blackburn and Appleton, Clifford and Manicur, or any combination of these individuals. Truly, they are different folks who use different strokes to reach the same objectives.

From these individuals we have evolved a collage of style which reveals the individual richness that emerges in given situations. Even though there has been an attempt to avoid too much personalization, those close to the authors will no doubt find identities behind the individual descriptions. Let the reader indulge himself or herself; the objective, however, is to present vignettes that offer cues to style that the reader may wish to test out in his or her own setting. The individual style cannot be successfully simulated: One man's feat is another man's folly. Nevertheless, from these glimpses may be drawn elements for one's own uniqueness and effectiveness in managing student affairs.

## The First Dean

His chancellor calls him one of the most skilled student affairs administrators he has known, and the principal reason is that he has a clear notion of the environment necessary for learning and the role that student affairs must play in shaping and improving that environment. Clarifying the mission of the institution is a high-priority objective. His manners are formal, evenly paced, and restrained; he exudes confidence but has a quiet means of expressing it. He has the capacity for acquiring competent staff and promotes their development. He is always thoroughly prepared, makes quiet but insistent demands on his staff, and wants solid data. In his own words: "It is the very worst thing to take hard, quick positions when one is dealing with conflicting issues. . . . Wait one day before sending the 'hot' memo." He respects integrity beyond all other traits. His personal life complements high professional standards. Admittedly, his considerate approach can be misinterpreted; he is cerebral more than emotional. His laughter may be a release from restraints, rather than an appreciative belly laugh. Nevertheless the highest respect flows easily from all colleagues. He can be characterized as an administrator's administrator. Anyone lacking in commitment would find it difficult to work with this dean.

> *Ordered, accountable, excellent on clarity of assignment or problem to be addressed, outwardly low-key but inwardly intense, supreme integrity, warm but seldom exciting, alert, friendly.*

## The Second Dean

This dean is probably in a class by himself. He would describe himself as a professional deviant, a stimulus not a response, a standard deviation from almost everyone. He is a fearless champion of what he believes; prejudice and pettiness, double-dealing, and calculating petulance are anathema to him. Exploitation enrages him. He particularly enjoys being the single dissenter in a discussion, and obviously relishes ruining a consensus—when he feels especially right on an issue. He is hardly the evocative leader who teases data from staff. Another dean says, "He speaks with such authority, he must be right." In his own words: "I am a paid, attractive nuisance; never an administrator, always a dean." He elicits strong emotion, stirs the adrenalin; certainly no one is neutral in thinking about him. He has few peers as a story teller, a raconteur of the ribald and the jocular. While he can finesse, his forte is to confront. This tends to put him in a position of high visibility, and one doubts that he minds. He views this visibility as an opportunity to teach. He enjoys interpersonal relationships but admits to enjoying helping people not as much as he enjoys using his mind to help people. His priorities are the goals of the institution, its academic standards and expectations, and only after these priorities are addressed does he turn his interests to students. Yet, he has been recognized for his ability to know every student on campus before the fall semester ends. He weaves his personal, social, and institutional lives into an impressive tapestry. His home has always been a hub of campus activity and a busy meeting place. Upon leaving one work assignment his campus paper carried the following headline: "Goodbye to a living legend." While he might cringe at the thought, it is clear that he is a sentimentalist. He has intense loyalties to those he trusts—may the rest beware!

> *Verbal, smiling, friendly, analytical, bold, contentious on principle, loyal, sociable for its sake, highly intelligent and curious.*

## The Third Dean

This dean enjoys extraordinary conceptual skills. To him deaning is leadership, not just being a processor. He is thoroughly formal, has been accused of wearing a tie with his pajamas. His enjoyable, warm personality belies a steely determination. His press for production may not always be supported by others. He talks and thinks rapidly, is fond of a clipped style of conveying ideas, and is capable of using profanity when he feels the situation warrants it. (Someone once observed that from him it does not sound like profanity.) He loves flair, yet is not putting on a show. He would rank among the top of the eight in innovative skills, is sought after as a consultant. On two campuses he has had a focal role in volatile issues covered by the national press. Both campuses benefited from his presence.

When the prize warrants, he is a risk taker. His leadership among professional colleagues has been conceptually exciting and intellectually challenging: New ground is always broken when he leads a group. His participation in staffs or on boards is worth emulating. The emphasis is always upon improvement, the refinement, even the replacement, of inadequate methods. Though he has been known to play the devil's advocate, his own integrity makes such a detour difficult to maintain for long. He can be aloof  but is protected by his sense of timing. He is fond of obstacles: "If obstacles are not obvious, you had better create some." He is forever on the prowl for information—reading, discussing, consulting. When he finds it, a memory as tenacious as his devotion to excellence seizes upon it.

*Intellectually aloof, informed, energetic; has definite causes, high commitment; hospitable and social, kindly, inventive; a pressure-cooker operator.*

## The Fourth Dean

This dean combines crisp humor and intellectual sophistication. He writes in paragraphs but speaks in phrases and crisp sentences that often

---

**His manner of speaking tends to make him quotable. He says that his style is predicated on the belief that:**

*You can run but you can't hide.*

*It is necessary to assume authority.*

*No one is keeping me from making contributions to teaching and learning except my own limitations; thus I am responsible both for what I do and don't do.*

*It is important to be dedicated but not compulsive. Humor is good for the soul; it respects neither rank nor privilege.*

*Trust is essential to all effective human relationships; in its absence control and/or authority emerge.*

*It is better to be intelligently ignorant than stupidly ignorant.*

*It is a waste of time to look for answers that are already within us.*

*Paternalism has gotten a bum rap.*

*One is well served in trusting the instincts of students.*

*It is OK to be a curmudgeon.*

*The number of people attending my funeral may well be determined by the weather.*

---

sound like proverbs. Few in the profession can match his lean prose and ordered presentation. More than one person has been found on the losing end of his double-entendres and deft jabs. One of our other eight deans believes this dean uses humor as a weapon, a means of unseating the pretentious. This may be true, but the writers have also seen this humor used as an alternative to abrasive conflict: It's hard to be angry when laughing. He does not wait upon ceremony but will act in anticipation of the approval of his superiors to remedy or prevent a problem before it gets out of hand. Some say he acts as though he is responsible to the whole university. An open-door dean, he must work at night to complete his university paperwork. He roams the campus and prefers first-hand observations to written reports. He really is not the gameskeeper of the academic preserve; yet, his vigilance is almost shepherd-like (this he might deny!). In his own words: "I would hope to be seen as reasonable, approachable, accessible, the kind of person who would put aside a piece of paper to talk with a student . . . of doing anything reasonable for a student, but not being conned."

## The Fifth Dean

This dean is the high-energy winner, sleeps a minimal number of hours, is a restless scholar. One guesses that he uses even his dream life to solve stubborn problems—trying out new options when his peers are satisfied with one or two sallies. He favors directness, appreciates solid arguments, and is an expert synthesizer. Equivocators make him nervous, and he shuns them every chance he gets. In complex discussions, he is usually the first to find the way to underlying principles and issues; admittedly, contrary opinions are not always heard. He is politically astute but is careful to win with the least possible expense to opponents. If controversy is lacking, he may introduce it. Where controversy exists, he will find a way to resolve it. His intensity frequently brings the need for rest, change, and new vistas. He is firm rather than friendly. While he enjoys people, he seems also to enjoy his privacy, spending time alone with his thoughts. He has an issue orientation, more than a people orientation, and most of his writing reflects this orientation. Enjoying exceptional memory, he has the capacity to reconstruct group conversations occurring years earlier, remembering who said what, and in what order.

> *Brief, crisp, nervously energetic, aggressive, candid (even to*
> *overdoing it), orderly of mind, quick on his feet, egoistic in*
> *the best sense (should have been born in Maine—Don't tread*
> *on me!), free, informed—no one owns him.*

## The Sixth Dean

In the effort to avoid personal identity, except to those who know the deans well, it seems too much a trick of the language to avoid the identity of NASPA's first woman president. She is also a high-energy person, has workaholic tendencies, yet is remarkably relaxed and unharried. Her exuberance is infectious, and her graciousness well known. Nonetheless, it is clear that her level of expectation is high and that one had better be prepared to deliver in working with her. She prefers to give her staff broad responsibilities, and the freedom to work unfettered. She exerts herself to achieve consensus, but lacking it, she will proceed if she believes her approach is right. She may emphasize process over purpose on a rare occasion. The dean readily shows her unhappiness with sloppy work, but her capacity for praise is equally quick and generous. She enjoys appropriate arrangements, a reflection of taste and high standards. She is an energetic student, enthusiastically absorbing the ideas of others, which she is capable of translating into her own style of work; understands the importance of detail but is never bogged down by it; leaves little to chance and would rather err on the side of over-preparedness. She has the capacity to elicit strong loyalty and responds in kind. Among her peers she has the Chief Dynamo title nailed down.

> *Prepared, even dogmatic at times, hard-working, more goal oriented than conceptual, courageous, neat, ordered, amiable, resolutely fair.*

## The Seventh Dean

This is the quiet dean, combining athletic ability, artistic flair, and a pervasive quality of integrity. He is not as verbally oriented as some of the other deans and does not appear to enjoy jousting for the sake of an argument. Sophisticated banter is as foreign to him as cheating in a footrace. It would be a waste of time to look for personal weakness in him. In talking with this dean, one feels in the presence of a truly religious man. He is capable of animation with an articulate left hand, especially as he talks about the symbolism of his sculptures, which abound in his home and office. Quiet joy is brought through the growth and maturity of a student or colleague; it can be seen in the deep sparkle in his eyes and a wide smile that applauds a student or colleague. Yet one can imagine him quite content to be alone working with his wood. Often he is asked to engage in issues that are difficult and sensitive, since he is essentially guileless. He avoids pejorative ways of speaking and behaving using his quiet sense of joy as his principal tool. Colleagues have noted his lack of vanity, his solid loyalty, and his genuine interest in others. In truth, such qualities are overwhelming, yet he could become a target of renegades. He avoids the political approach, but this tends to make him a superb, if somewhat vulnerable, politican.

*Never superficial, strong, patient, kindly, artistic, unyielding, fair, will not take advantage of anyone— almost apolitical.*

## The Eighth Dean

The last in this list of deans may be as youthful, as energetic and athletic, as happily involved at 70 as he is now. The bounce of his stride belies boundless physical resources which support a probing, optimistic, and issue-oriented mind. In organization life he has been a builder, an innovator and adventurous experimenter, a solidly responsible group and association leader. Away from the office he is a respected parent, a perceptive friend.

Another of his strengths lies in his ease of sharing his energies and his enthusiasm in constructive participation. He deplores stand-offishness, is usually into the issue or fray before many are aware of it. His predominant strength comes in exciting and stimulating exchange and in resolution of issues, ideas, and approaches. He makes friends easily, often as co-adventurers or colleagues in challenging situations. He believes that important relationships are mutually rewarding, even to the point of some vulnerability. He is always to be reckoned with, not as an aggressive opponent, but as one whose actions and ideas may preempt the field.

He is politically savvy, yet will refuse to let self-interest intrude too much. Elitism is frowned upon. His commitment to stated principles is total; his tone is religious in quality, his tactics statesmanlike, the product positive and practical. He reasons with and does not impose upon others. Only infrequently does he lead by directive: Nonetheless, he is aggressive, though he might not admit it. His easy manner belies a tenaciousness and participation intentions are sometimes unreconciled with demand for control. The emerging esprit de corps is convincing evidence of his leadership. All this occurs in a friendly exchange. Making others feel important is an aspect of style. He can accomplish as much with a chuckle as with a challenge.

*Fast on his feet, heavy on planning and follow-up, exemplar in confidence-building and in eliciting performance from others, issue-conscious, quick synthesizer in formal or casual settings.*

## Commonalities of Style

Through this collage of style may be viewed the unique behavior of these deans—what works for them. At the same time, some common features of style are apparent among the eight. Without implying that these commonalities of style, or the traits revealed which influence the styles, will guarantee success for anyone, they may bear emulation in the development of one's own personal style.

### INSTITUTIONAL LOYALTY

Some readers may rail in learning that deep loyalty to and feeling for the individual institution they serve is an important factor in the developing style of the dean. In some instances, the view is anthropomorphic: "To me the University is like a person; when it suffers, I suffer." None report a "company store" point of view, however, as each of them has had to criticize the institution at one or another time. It would seem that the feeling the deans have for the campus is a function of the emotional investments they have made in the institution. Yet, the strong commitment is also to the understood educational objectives and the teaching mission of the campus. This institutional loyalty also carries with it the belief that few important responsibilities can be carried out without cooperation among the bureaucratic units that make up the academic, extracurricular, and administrative whole of their respective institutions.

### LIVING WITH AMBIGUITY

Events that command our attention are typically beyond our ability to control. The present demands our time, but the future occupies our thoughts and hopes. We must cope with hundreds (over the years, thousands) of individuals participating in our lives, individuals having their own unique values, histories, and ways of perceiving. Life's ambiguities are endless but bear on the expectations others have of us, and of expectations we have for ourselves.

All of the deans acknowledged the anxieties born of uncertainty. They have learned to accept uncertainty, have adapted to it, have attempted to use it to good ends. The deans do not have a fatalistic view, as easy as that might be; they seem to be genuinely convinced of the importance of their full effort and participation, even while recognizing that life may be neither understandable, reasonable, nor fair; but they feel that positive growth and change are just as likely outcomes of the unknown future. Several commented on the quest for certainty they see in students, thus they believe it is important that they convey the promise of living fully in an era of uncertainty. They are not naive; they seem quite aware that life's surprises can be friendly or unfriendly, but one must live completely in any case.

Loyalty to the institution and to the learning process itself dominates the style of the deans. Yet, their own values and needs of students are not sacrificed. In fact, they recognize that strong allegiance to the mission of the institution, their own values, and the needs of students are not always easily reconciled. There is adventure and challenge, yes ambiguity, in trying to mesh these variables under some of the circumstances in which they find themselves. They occasionally find it necessary to live with ambiguity for various periods of time, with one foot in what is considered good by the institution and the other in what is regarded as necessary by the students.

### STUDENTS

It is clear that the deans enjoy their relationships with students, individually or in groups. Although they often serve as student advocates, they will try to look at the substance of the total issue before deciding upon a position or action. They tend to advocate their own positions—filtered through an understanding of the institutional mission, professional principles, and then an understanding of student values and needs. Their close identification with students makes advocacy possible in typical situations. The most anguishing problems, clearly, involve instances when students and the institution itself are at odds. Deans across the nation will find that dilemma familiar. According to one dean, ". . . I seek opportunities for students to advocate for themselves, to have an impact on policies and procedures which affect their lives, and to share in the creation of a humane environment on the campus. They must be heard whether or not they are heeded."

## CONSEQUENCES FOLLOW BEHAVIOR

The deans seem acutely aware that what they do (or what they fail to do) may affect the lives of others, and the overall environment of their campuses. It is also clear that the deans regard themselves as their own most valued advisers. This is not just the ego at work but represents rather a

> I am not a student advocate. Some student affairs administrators run around with a blank sheet of paper asking students what they ought to believe in. I hope I am an advocate of the educational objectives of the institution. If the two coincide, then I am a student advocate; I am not just a messenger of student opinion.—Blackburn

belief that one shapes events in the most personal way possible. There is a sense of aloneness (not to be mistaken for "lonely") among several of the eight, even though their interpersonal skills are excellent. There is a democratic tendency in the group, but it has its limits. If they need assistance in considering how to proceed, they will not hesitate to seek it, but, once having decided, will do so without further advice. To defend a position, one must be intellectually in charge when the decision is made.

## STAFF DEVELOPMENT

Most of the deans show the security to attract strong colleagues. The eight deans seem particularly proud of their staffs, and are pleased about their relationships with both past and present staffs. Though there are substantial differences in the degree to which formal staff experiences and programs are planned, all share the view that significant and expanding responsibilities on-the-job are the critical features of staff development. Staff development is a constant secondary objective played out along with other responsibilities.

## CHANGE AS A RESULT OF ENCOUNTER

It may seem presumptuous to the reader, though it did not to the interviewer, that the deans believe persons should be affected as a result of interaction with them. The eight affirm they have something of worth to contribute, whether it be information, direction, values, insights, or whatever is called for in a given circumstance. They seem to be value-explicit in these encounters, though sensitive of imposing their views on others. As one dean put it: "If I can't come up with better reasons for a student to behave differently than his reason for continuing as he is, then

**We have a prime responsibility to mobilize people resources and to create a sense of worth in staff personnel. It is the leader's responsibility to help staff mesh their own goals and objectives with those of the institution.—Appleton**

either he is right or I am inadequate." Some deans prefer very direct approaches, while others favor indirection. Human encounters, regardless of one's approach, are seen as opportunities for teaching, and no one seeks to avoid them, though they are not always pleasant. It is also clear that relationships of this kind are seen as mutually rewarding, with the dean growing as well.

### HUMILITY

Is humility any less for talking about it? While there are certainly no ego-deficiencies among the eight, one is struck by the overarching sense of humility in each. They recognize the frail threads which keep them on the job, and the ease by which these threads can be cut. All seem to enjoy their work, but this does not take the form of arrogance. Besides liking what they do, the deans like to talk about it. Yet, a sense of humility, an abiding respect for others, and an appreciation of the opportunities they enjoy, are common traits. One suspects that a recognition of the fragility of their circumstances accounts for part of these views.

### DO NOT TAKE SELF TOO SERIOUSLY

The interview results reveal frequent references to laughter, and the deans laughed at themselves in recounting campus anecdotes. Some of this laughter was self-deprecating, but not too costly. One dean cited a familiar axiom: "Take your job seriously but not yourself." "If I died on

information-oriented, though their preferences for gaining information are different. Some like to read, some would prefer first-hand observation. They appear to be looking for staffs who also have this orientation. One of the eight remarked: "I have a subconscious inclination to say 'yes' to program changes. I know that we cannot be satisfied with what we are currently doing." This should not translate as change-for-change-sake. The deans are resource-conscious, and seek ways of doing more with steady-state dollars.

### ADMINISTRATION AS A BATTING AVERAGE

In response to a faculty colleague who wondered how the dean was bearing up under some criticism by the school paper, the dean noted, "They're going to have to take me on my batting average." Anyone serving in the field for any length of time is going to receive criticism, will be second-guessed, and cannot hope to uniformly please the whole spectrum of critics and observers abounding on almost any campus issue. It seems to be a challenge for those deans to pick and choose those items in which winning is important—"selective neglect" orders their very busy days.

The deans show an intellectual understanding of criticism, but they still chafe somewhat in receiving it, particularly when they feel the criticism is unfair. Resilience seems to rescue all of them, as they indicate that the present controversy will pass, only to have another one emerge: "That's the way it is; if you can't tolerate it, you can't survive," says one of the group.

---

If I do not care about winning, I will compromise; if the goal is important, then the picture is different.—Blackburn

---

## A Summation

We have attempted, briefly, to illustrate something of the styles of the eight deans, and the factors impinging on those styles which are commonly seen as important. To mimic would be an error; to use these materials to reflect on one's own style is our objective. The overall thesis remains, however: the uniqueness which each dean brings to the job. The deans seem to have a perspective which sustains them across all kinds of issues, over the many years they have served. They understand their opportunities and their limitations. Their perspective may be illustrated by the poet, Laotzu:

> Those who would take over the earth
> And shape it to their will
> Never, I notice, succeed.
> The earth is like a vessel so sacred
> That at the mere approach of the profane
> It is marred
> And when they reach out their fingers it is gone.
> For a time in the world some force themselves ahead
> And some are left behind.
> For a time in the world some make a great noise
> And some are held silent,
> For a time in the world some are puffed fat
> And some are kept hungry,
> For a time in the world some push aboard
> And some are tipped out:
> At no time in the world will a man who is sane
> Over-reach himself,
> Over-spend himself,
> Over-rate himself.

## References

Adler, A. The Fundamental Views of Individual Psychology. *International Journal of Individual Psychology*. 1935. In Hall, C. and Lindzey, G. *Theories of Personality*. New York: John Wiley and Sons, Inc., 1957.

Cleland, D.J. and King, W. *Systems Analysis and Project Management*. New York: McGraw-Hill Book Co., 1968, pp. 12-15.

Laotzu. *The Way of Life*. (Eittner, Bynner, trans.). New York: John Day, 1944, p. 43.

# Our Future Is Showing

*This space voyage is totally precarious. We depend upon a little envelope of soil and a rather larger envelope of atmosphere for life itself. And both can be contaminated and destroyed. . . . We are a ship's company on a small ship. Rational behavior is the condition of survival . . .*

*Yet rational rules of behavior are what we largely lack. . . . Can we take some of the energy and imagination, some of the vision and hard work that are forcing us together in so many fields and use them . . . to build the institutions of a decent human society? Can we convert casual physical proximity into the city of man?*

*The plain truth is that if we cannot, as a human community, create the institutions of civilized living, our chances of carrying on the human experiment are just about nil. This is no longer hyperbole; it is no longer rhetoric or cliches; it is simple fact.*

*—Barbara Ward, Spaceship Earth*

ENTER THE UNIVERSITY, a microcosm of American society, itself one of the more enlightened clubs in the shrinking megapolis that is the world. In the University, faculty, students, and other denizens of longer or shorter duration have the opportunity to review the accomplishments of the past and the prospects for the future, to organize and channel unused reservoirs of talent, to bring about important breakthroughs toward the replacement of the lonely crowd with the shared community.

With luck, those who draw mostly upon the past will be able to affect enough of those normally concerned about the future—their own, certainly, and, it is hoped, the future of those they can influence in the changing cycles of their lives—to turn the course of human affairs from unproductive introspection and warping self-concern to a broader interest in helping others on our shrinking turf.

Under the model projected in this book, the harvest of graduates prepared to look at society more than self may be increased; their internships in learning to live with university peers may be translated into internships in learning to live in the larger society; and the university may have resumed a function that has been dominated in latter years by career at the expense of community.

The promise of such transformation, of which Barbara Ward is only one of the growing number of earnest, if not frantic, seekers, lies as much in the student affairs area as in any area of higher learning. However they may have been perceived by whatever segment of the campus, student personnel administrators have been the major proponents and practitioners of community in higher education. And further, what is clear, is that the future of student affairs is inextricably tied to what is the future direction of higher education.

---

**Authors' Advice To Aspiring Administrators:**

*"Hurry, I'd like to retire!"*

*"Visit a psychiatrist."*

*"It becomes such a part of your life . . . get out unless you're excited."*

*"Be willing to walk away at any time."*

*"Show a willingness to take positions with lesser titles in order to diversify."*

---

We can only affirm that in the next few decades, the pairing of realistic, provocative student affairs concepts and practices with rebirth of core curricula and a restored concern for excellence in all American education could contribute much to the materials and the making of that fragile web we call community, so critical to our continued human existence as to rival life itself in importance.

## Whence Comes Genius? Wisdom?

Would Einstein have promulgated his theories if he hadn't received a university education? The world has known primitive geniuses who have made spectacular contributions to basic knowledge and theoretical science. Einstein may have been among them; he may have contributed greatly, though unschooled, but the contributions would have been slower and fewer, and his total production would likely have been far short of what it became with his grooming at Zurich.

Whether the world needs genius more than effective, earnest scholars with an affinity for service as much as for inquiry, only the future can tell. The chances are that both genius and knowledge, with an unlimited source of wisdom thrown in, will be needed in abundance in the years ahead, unless the world retrogresses to its brute origins, a not unlikely fate if it fails to produce some social geniuses along with its great technicians and researchers in industry and science.

---

**Authors' Advice to Aspiring Administrators:**

*"Be sure to prepare for alternative careers . . . the opportunities may not be as secure in the 80s; certainly less mobility and fewer promotions may be predicted."*

*"Mobility will be enhanced if the aspiring dean is articulate, widely read, viewed as an educational person rather than a technician."*

*"The hazard of overwork is ever present. The job is never done . . . selective neglect must be carefully practiced."*

---

Few will dispute that, as in the past, the intellectual fecundity and fertility needed to counter social, cultural, and cerebral decline will be found in our colleges and universities. Education is a major source of an intelligent citizenry, a civilized society, and an effective, creative, work force. Institutions of higher education should bear the brunt of this responsibility, aided of course by family, other institutions of society such as the church, the media and the market place.

How might higher education anticipate the full burden of the coming years? First, it must realize that society will expect more, not less, from its campuses, although at the same time saying in effect, Do *more* with *less*. Those institutions of higher education that accept the challenge to do more, to support renowned faculty, to press on in search of answers to society's ills—mental, social, cultural, physical—will not face the withdrawal pains that the less community-conscious will experience when funding dries up. "Business as usual" translates to "the way we used to do it" rather quickly in a society whose dynamics—negative or positive—are constantly accelerating. Second, higher education must stop its preoccupation with "the diminishing pool of freshmen in the 1980s" and focus on the changing age picture on most campuses: from the traditional predominance of students 18 to 23 years old to a more sophisticated, multi-faceted range from 20 to 70 or more.

For whatever reason, growth in enrollment could continue indefinitely if costs can be kept down and classroom space available. But the students will not all be the unsophisticated freshmen; many will be adults from a variety of maturing and altering environments, seeking knowledge, to be sure, but also seeking professional redirection, personal enrichment, social and emotional repair, a host of other objectives increasingly seen in community colleges, continuing education, and liberal arts colleges. A critical question for student administrators of whatever depth or variety of experience, now on the scene or standing in the wings: Will the older student bring a different set of needs and wants? The answer: The institution that has kept pace with our changing culture today with a staff that is not afraid to take the bit, no matter the pace or track, is far more likely to survive and serve that unprobed influx than one that continues to do business as usual. These students may be mediocre or model parents, excellent craftsmen or all thumbs, political office holders or uninvolved citizens. Yet, they are meeting and talking with each other—educating peers and professors as well as themselves.

Though the final measure that society may apply is a university's ability to inculcate employable qualities and skills, not how to get along with your neighbor or yourself, the university must try to educate for life at least in the same proportion as it educates for livelihood.

In the years since World War II the university too often has gone along with the pragmatist in accepting as a major, if not the primary, responsibility the preparation of individuals for jobs and careers. With the majority, the differences between professional preparation and vocational training are mainly those of status rather than objective. The effect upon even some of our greatest institutions of higher learning has been to reduce them almost to occupational shopping centers, diminishing their historic role of exemplifying and exalting learning and of serving the human concerns that are the very force and fiber of life.

But if interest in liberal arts is sloping downward, and even the Ph.D's are queuing up for ever-scarcer openings for ever-increasing numbers of graduates, what is the university's proper role? Without a major shift in society's as well as its own perception, the university cannot divest itself of the role it increasingly serves, that of a kind of occupational public utility rather than a resource for learning to live effectively in the human community. By its nature and its heritage, the university is the vehicle for the past, present, and future impedimenta and scintilla of civilization, but its latter-day driver has been the University Placement Agency. With such a driver, who is headed in all directions, there can be no good and sufficient road map except the very arts and skills of living itself.

In its truest form, the university is obligated to inculcate and refine these arts and skills—to provide understandings, experiences, and challenges designed to acquaint students with their world, as well as with their imminent occupational cubicles. Intelligent corporate officers want applicable skills, certainly, but on the corporate growth path on which they place their most promising new hires they look deeper—for creativity, the ability to conceptualize, social skills, a degree of venturesomeness, emotional competence, courage in decision-making, and the ability to talk knowledgeably about something besides GNP, data points, and energy alternatives.

---

**Authors' Advice to Aspiring Administrators:**

*"Don't forget to dream. When the flow of new ideas or the pace of dreams slows, the end is in sight."*

*"Job satisfaction must be related to factors other than regular promotion to new and broader positions, because this is not happening routinely."*

*"Be willing to understand that the dean often moves toward insecurity, not more security, at the top."*

---

As often as not, students trying to achieve these qualities are hindered or even obstructed by academic fiefdoms, commonly called departments, which use the weapon of the asterisk (denoting required course) to joust with other fiefdoms or baronies for space, staff, and clout. The student forced to yield to the Man with the Asterisk becomes increasingly disenchanted by yet another obstacle in his or her stumbling preparation for life and for work.

The message here is that the university must resume some or all of its traditional concerns for, not just livelihood, but living. As the Chancellor of one of our authors noted, "It is the last, not the first job held by a graduate which should drive our institutions."

The examples of the eight administrators represented in this book indicated a common thrust for exposing students and staff to interactive, mutually enriching exchange that will enhance our living forces and our living styles; they exemplify not administrative mechanics but a celebration of the total person whose goal is not only better paychecks but a better way to live and work with himself and others.

---

**Authors' Advice to Aspiring Administrators:**

*"I have a continuing regret that there is never time to relish what you have done right."*

*"One's life cannot be lived as a preoccupation for tasks that other people think are important. Some days it is important to sit back in the chair and say, 'I did all these things that nobody but myself knows about. What impact did I have, and what price did I pay?' And if I concluded that nobody gave a tinker's damn for all of that unseen effort, I would ask myself, 'Would I do it again?' And I would say, 'You're damn right I would.'*

*"That's integrity."*

---

Their rationales, their commitments to good practices, their stamina, strategy, and stimulation as administrative "playing coaches," if you will, and their unanimous concern for student and staff growth are the main strands and hues of the collective administrative tapestry woven in this book. And the future deans will not exist so much because of unique organizational structures or administrative portfolios, but because of their personal and professional qualities and an institutional commitment to livelihood *and* life.

## The Awakening

No matter their zeal or their techniques, the bridge between teachers and students—whether matriculating sophomore or veteran staff colleague—is based upon that ineffable element sometimes called the teachable moment. Isn't this what we're advocating for our institutions?

Martin Buber in *Between Man and Man* suggests when that moment comes:

> *When the pupil's confidence has been won, his resistance against being educated gives way to a singular happening: He accepts the educator as a person. He feels he may trust this man, that this man is not making a business out of him but is taking part in his life, accepting him before desiring to influence him . . .*

> *Confidence, of course, is not won by the strenuous endeavor to win it, but by direct and ingenuous participation in the life of the people one is dealing with—in this case in the life of one's pupils—and by assuming the responsibility which arises from that participation. It is not the educational intention but it is the personal meeting itself which is educationally fruitful.*

## References

Buber, M. *Between Man and Man*. New York: Beacon Press, 1955.

Ward, B. *Spaceship Earth*. New York: Columbia University Press, 1966.

# Memo to the President

Office of the President
De Loema Center

Dr. Agnes Webb
Professor, English Literature
Beta State University

Dear Dr. Webb:

I appreciate your willingness to chair the University
Task Force on Student Life. There exist a number of
fundamental issues with respect to student life at Beta
State which it is apparent are not being addressed
adequately. I anticipate hearing from you.

Sincerely,

*J.M. Marshall*

J.M. Marshall
President

JMM:sp

TO:                 President J.M. Marshall

FROM:             Agnes Webb,  Professor, English Literature
                        *aw*
SUBJECT:        Interim Report, Task Force on Student Life

I know that you have been under persistent pressure from the Board, students, and the press, to respond to the several issues which became the charge of my committee. I can report that all ten members have worked diligently these past several months to come up with some recommendations that will be useful to you and to the students and faculty you serve.

Even so, I must report that we are as yet unprepared to report out a set of recommendations. We have made substantial diagnostic progress, but we face several difficult dilemmas that must be resolved before we can act with confidence as a total group. I told you as much last week, and you indicated that an interim report would be very helpful.

Since our visit, I have pulled together notes gathered from various sources. The enclosed notes are not inclusive, but rather represent some areas discussed to date. On some of them *substantial* discussion has taken place. I am excited about the task you have assigned us but doubt that we can make a final report this year.

Your letter to us anticipated very well the problems we have in fact encountered, dealing with some central issues concerning the University's stewardship in meeting the full range of educational needs of our students. I have chuckled on occasion in realizing that even this—the most distinguished blue ribbon committee I have been part of—has at times been unable to arrive at a consensus on what a "university education" should embody.

One segment clearly sees our responsibility in historical terms, involving the intellectual activity of classroom, laboratory, and library. They understand the functions of education to be the preservation, transmission, and enrichment of the important elements of our culture, brought about through teaching and research. This in itself is far more complex than I can report here, but is in contrast to those who accept the basic definition but wish to broaden its parameters.

A group of our faculty believe that emotional and physical aspects of growth deserve more attention, that these dimensions of life are in fact inseparable from the cognitive elements that have traditionally occupied our time and attention. The latter group would argue that human development would be improved by a more integrated effort (cognitive, affective, psychomotor experiences) occurring in an environment which encouraged all three.

This critical concern has yet to be resolved by our committee. Admittedly, it is at first glance abstract, but in the concrete issues I cite you can pick up the specifics of the dilemma. Perhaps it can be simply put by asking: What responsibilities can our faculty realistically be expected to handle? The pressure of teaching and research, in addition to the tremendous amount of student-related committee work every faculty member is asked to perform, result in assignments that some very well-meaning faculty are beginning to see as an unrelenting burden. In fact, even the most dedicated, seeing more, non-academic responsibilities coming their way as a result of our study, would call it a rank imposition.

One conclusion is certain: Our present approach is unsatisfactory and must be adjusted. The needs of students are not being met, as presently will be shown. Faculty (those interested in this issue) are working hard but are frustrated. Of course, student unhappiness is the principal reason you formed the committee.

As you instructed, I have attempted in the following paragraphs to avoid the abstract, philosophical questions, as important as they are, and have stressed concrete issues and problems. They are not arranged in any particular order, but to the extent that I was able to group the issues I have done so.

1. *Our Diversity of Interests, Needs, and Perceptions*—In looking at a summary of student perceptions of BSU, one wonders at times if they are all talking about the same campus, in fact about this campus at all. They see us so much differently from the way we see ourselves. No doubt this is due in part to the unique personal characteristics each student brings to us. Clearly, their differing predispositions and perceptions have some relevance to the kind of educational experience students will (or will not) receive. The

campus community could benefit from a more refined awareness of the impact of the varying levels of development, values, interests, etc., which students bring to us. We must pursue this understanding more vigorously than we have to date.

2. *A Census of Our Environments Needed*—The total collection of personalities we have on the campus contributes to a kind of dynamic environment, different from that of any other campus, yet similar in many ways. Students respond to that environment, and surely the environment is in constant flux as it absorbs or is affected by those in its midst. One committee member astutely observed that one of our major tasks is to identify as many of our subcultures as feasible, and to attempt to assess their importance. The person/environment interaction is a phenomenon which psychologists are well aware of, but frankly it is a matter which most of us know very little about. We should find someone to help us define and articulate these manifestations and what they might mean here at BSU. (Perhaps the Faculty Research Committee could expand its role.)

3. *The Varieties of Learning*—You are aware that Martha Reynolds, Psychology, is a member of the Committee. Some of her insights have been most interesting. It is quite apparent to me, as a teacher in the humanities, that much of what she knows in a technical sense about how, why, and when students learn, I know in quite different ways to be true. Unfortunately, I don't know why it is true, nor can I always follow her patient efforts to explain learning theories to the committee. It is clear that some committee members are not particularly interested in these questions, but I see them both as fascinating and of potential usefulness. I have been a faculty member here for 18 years, Reynolds for 10, and yet I was not at all aware of her remarkable grasp of students and the various processes of learning that affect their academic and social progress. And I doubt that she would know, because I have never had an occasion to tell her, that I know she is right, but for *my* reasons! This lament is not without an essential point: Faculty must find ways to interact with each other for the good impact it may have on the teaching skills each will take back to the classroom. It seems ironic that when dollars are getting tighter we are failing to utilize potentials among us which cost nothing but our time and attention.

4. *"Faculty Development" and Our Personnel Files*—Our faculty development program may be useful in this context. I am embarrassed to admit that I have not yet found time to participate. Probably I am one of those holding an unfair view that participation in "faculty development" means one is admitting shortcomings in working with students. I think you should know that some junior faculty do not participate because they feel such participation might actually be held against them as they proceed toward promotion and tenure. I think we need to divorce this activity from the Provost's office altogether. I know the Provost's attitudes are good, but faculty are wary of trotting out their shortcomings if they feel that such admissions will find their way to faculty folders and deans' offices.

5. *Our Faculty As Recruiters Incidentally*—The method we have used for explaining the institution to students across the state is becoming very difficult. To ask faculty to travel as much as they have to in order to do this job correctly is a demand almost everyone sees as impractical. Students have complained about professorial absences, faculty do not want to be away from their families for extended periods of time, and the information needed by faculty is often beyond what they appear to possess. If we are going to continue with this pattern, some kind of model approach will have to be developed. We are running into contradictions, poor information, and other lapses that relate directly to a lack of preparation, as much as I hate to report that to you. We are not always equipped to pass along basic information in a timely and concise manner. It may well be that a faculty member (or several) should consider doing this full-time, say for a year or so, rotating the assignment as necessary. I think the committee believes that the first "window" we offer to the campus is not always good, which is truly unfortunate in light of the overall excellence of our academic programs.

6. *Campus Visits, Good and Bad*—Similarly, prospective student visits to the campus are very poorly coordinated. Some truly embarrassing situations have occurred. We don't want to single out any department. It is fair to say that some departments do an exceptionally fine job and some hurt us tremendously by their

inexplicable attitudes. I think that we will be recommending the creation of a Faculty Visitation Committee, charged with the responsibility of coordinating the several necessary activities involved when prospective students and their parents come to visit. It seems to the committee that we must learn to accommodate the single student just as we attempt to serve larger numbers coming on high school-sponsored trips. It is obvious that disserving even one prospective student results in unfortunate generalizing, with bad echoes reaching we know not how far. You will need additional detail on this, which I am not in a position to supply now.

7. *Our Graphic Information Is Suspect*—A corollary to the recruiting/admissions process is the written information we disseminate. It is at least uneven and often very poor in quality, by anyone's standards. As a professor of literature, I don't even want to know who wrote some of that material. The artwork is primitive, which is a pity since the graphic arts department is one of our best. Why aren't they involved in preparing our handbooks and brochures? I think the message we convey through the use of this substandard material is not a good one, and I doubt that you will find many faculty colleagues who disagree. We believe the skill is available, but it apparently will have to be coaxed out or organized.

8. *Financial Aid Area Weak*—A particularly grievous limitation of our recruiting faculty is their inability to deal in a straightforward manner with the questions involving financial aids for prospective students. We seem to be particularly inept in this area, and I know that parents have brought this to your attention. I regret to say that I must point to the Central National Bank people in this regard. If their contract for administering our financial aids program is due for renewal, I believe we should look for another resource. They are slow in making awards, and we are not sure that they are honoring the policy positions set by the Faculty Committee on Financial Aids. I will refer to this problem again later.

9. *Admissions Processing Lags*—I must also report our concern about the lag-time in processing admissions on the campus. The Faculty Committee on Admissions is large, and I realize members are having a hard time getting together. Their subcommittee approach

may be the answer, but it is too soon to tell. As we understand it, Arcadia State is using an outside firm, Associated Personnel Services, a firm which screens applicants for business and industry. I would find that approach distasteful, but the ASU people seem both relieved and happy to have it. One must also note that their enrollment is up again this year, though perhaps there are other reasons.

10. *Is Our Orientation "Sterile"?*—Another program that contributes to student impressions is orientation. There is a uniform view that our program falls far short of what is needed. "Sterile" is one of the friendlier descriptions offered by the committee. Members feel that the reasons are fairly clear: The junior faculty who run the program are practically conscripted. Few senior faculty participate at all. This causes understandable resentments, and the mental set of the junior faculty is so negative that they have not seen the potential value of a good program. Our materials, again, are not adequate. Someone raised the possibility of using faculty spouses to do this work, and we will give that some thought. In any case, extra pay for this work might make it more attractive. As it is, poor attitudes by faculty cannot help but influence the attitudes of newly enrolled students. The new transfer student is a special case of the above. It is clear that their needs differ from those of freshmen, but we make no such differentiation in our orientation offerings.

11. *Little Done With Parents*—A recurring theme in our committee conversations dealt with how little we are doing with parents. For all practical purposes they are being left out of the entire collegiate experience, and we feel this is both regrettable and avoidable. We will be suggesting the development of some kind of vehicle for communicating with parents; our first effort is to get them informed, and then to get them involved. We believe some very positive untapped potential exists in this area. Orientation would be the logical place to establish parent contacts.

12. *Advisement A Major Concern*—The integration of academic advising with more general orientation goals was a wise decision in principle. Some of the problems we have encountered are due to junior faculty, as noted above, but additional comments seem required. As you are well aware, we are striving to enroll students who plan

to seriously pursue their studies. It is clear, however, that we have overestimated a typical student's ability to declare a major with any certainty. Information reviewed by the committee reveals 20,000 occupational titles in the United States. While these can be narrowed rapidly, to a point, it gets increasingly difficult as one continues to narrow the final choices. It is obvious that many intelligent 18-year-old students cannot narrow their choices sufficiently. At least this has been the experience of our campus. The more intelligent the student, the more options available. Academic advising must take these circumstances into account, rather than each college seeking to fatten its enrollment. Many students do not have either the experience or the maturity to decide on a major. I think the committee has come to realize that "undecided" means a great deal more than we might have thought as we began our deliberations. Incidentally, we have experienced excellent success with one course offered by the Social Science faculty which is specifically concerned with career exploration and which undecided students can take for credit. There are real differences on the committee with respect to this potential innovation, and there is some concern about its expansion: Basically, do we have enough faculty equipped to teach such a course if expanded? Also, the notion of providing credit toward graduation for such courses is one that will meet opposition from some departments.

13. *Part-Time Work Program Needed*—Some preliminary conversation occurred that focused on the possibility of arranging for part-time work experiences which might bear on eventual career choices. There are instances of that elsewhere, of course, but I did not sense much enthusiasm for getting into that here. This would seem to require significant coordination from a variety of sources, and I think that while the goal is applauded the practical problems are too overwhelming for us right now. In reference to our present part-time work situation, I call your attention to a serious problem we presently see with our confused, if not nonexistent, policy. As you are aware, we post part-time jobs on designated campus bulletin boards. We may need to discontinue this practice. Unauthorized listings can be found on nearly every bulletin board; many listings are old, and no one takes them down; we feel that some new listings are torn off so that other students can't get them

until the student removing the posting has had a crack at the job; few employers call to indicate the jobs that are filled (even if they did, we might not be able to find the listings). But perhaps the greatest reason for discontinuing this service is blatantly discriminatory behavior. We find that some employers will not hire women, indicating "male only" right on the listing, and of course this cannot be tolerated. Minority students are also vulnerable in these cases. Even though we do not screen listings, I doubt that we want to play even a peripheral helping role to employers acting this way. This service, with all its faults, is still valuable to some students, but our thinking at the moment is that the problems outweigh the benefits.

14. *Our Attrition Rate Needs Analysis*—We are trying to better understand the rate of attrition that is occurring for any number of reasons. We do not feel well informed at this point, but it is clear that academic problems are frequently uncovered after it is impossible to do much about them. A means for earlier detection is needed, though we are not sure of the mechanism.

15. *Remedial Program Indicated*—A related issue involves the remedial needs of students, those having skills deficiencies resulting from their high school experience. While faculty are not enthused about this situation, they recognize the importance of upgrading these skills. Reading, writing, and mathematics deficiencies are common, and students are reporting considerable concerns about their overall study habits. We have some faculty devoting time to these areas, but I believe they will not be able to sustain this activity over any length of time, given their other responsibilities. It seems clear that this is a crucial area, however, and it needs more attention.

16. *Self-Assessment Techniques Considered*—One way of dealing with the above issues, along with some to follow, is to teach self-assessment techniques to students, across a range of issues. The instruments are apparently available, but someone must help students learn to interpret results. This would seem to be a viable idea; it would put the responsibility where it probably belongs. But someone is going to have to take some initial responsibility in this area.

17. *Paraprofessional Program Feasible?*—This reminds me that student members of the committee feel quite strongly that students can serve in much more useful ways in some of these areas. They believe they could very easily serve as a kind of paraprofessional resource for their younger and/or newer peers. There is a difference of opinion on the committee both as to whether this might work and/or whether it is a good idea in general. It is my opinion that, in our final report, we will strongly recommend that use of student paraprofessionals, under good supervision, will be both economically sound and educationally valuable.

18. *Beyond the Cognitive*—As we look toward the revamping of our general education curriculum, it may be timely to look at a series of issues ranging beyond the cognitive. Creativity, assertion, love are terms that come to mind. One direction suggested by these concerns involves women, particularly more mature women. About 70 per cent of our enrollment growth the past two years is due to the increase in women students. They report any number of unique problems. Some have great difficulty with child care needs. Some of them are afraid that they cannot compete with younger students; some are not getting much encouragement from their husbands. The women report an interest in forming groups to talk about these issues, and both men and women faculty are supportive but are already spread thin with other responsibilities. If a program could be devised, it would illustrate in one very concrete way how affective and cognitive issues merge in the educational lives of these students.

19. *Personal Improvement Opportunities*—It may seem preposterous to some, in considering our responsibilities to students, that some students want to form groups to deal with preparation for marriage, human sexuality, marital issues, etc., some of which relate to student issues and some of which do not. Someone has even offered the view that we should provide a program helping passive people to be more assertive! What next!

20. *Religious Interests*—Religious issues represent another possibility for integrating general scholarship and important human issues operating in the daily lives of students. We have a long way to go in this area, as the Religion department is extremely conservative in

its approach to scholarship. I don't think that I will want to be the one to invite them to participate in the development of programs focusing on the religious experience. They will probably recommend a guru for all of us. Nonetheless, this issue is an important one for individual students seeking to find an avenue of expression for their religious concerns. It seems unwise to just ignore this issue and simply refer students to local churches. Surely this is a matter of sufficient importance for us to consider.

21. *Minority Student Interests*—A number of minority students seem to have the same problems as the student body at large—and then some. If minority students come to Beta from predominately Black or Chicano high schools, participating in this campus is difficult. There are very few minority faculty, and there are distinct cultural, if not racial, differences among us which keep tensions rather high. Improvement here requires the attention—maybe full-time—of some of us.

22. *Economic Backgrounds Viewed*—There is growing evidence that college achievement is influenced by economic status. Certainly we have a large number of students from low income backgrounds, but as far as I know we are doing nothing specifically in their behalf. This was noted by the committee; some faculty, however, see our present position as a wholly defensible, egalitarian position. One argued that low-income students would be offended if set apart in any way.

23. *Students and Their Financial Needs*—The item above reminds me again of our financial aids dilemma. The Central National Bank people are at odds both with the Faculty Financial Aids people and many students. Are you aware that students without a credit rating are getting unfavorable financial aid reviews from the banks? Some low-income students have never been in a bank. We have learned that one needy student was disqualified for aid because he had written a check for insufficient funds at a local department store. We need to ask who is in charge of this program. A related issue in financial aids has to do with overdue loans. Central National people have asked faculty to call students out of class and are applying pressure that some faculty feel is inappropriate to a higher education setting. I believe that faculty members are becoming increasingly restive with this arrangement; it interferes

with classroom relationships. I doubt that we can be permitted to serve as bill collectors, even in the most peripheral way.

24. *Veterans Need Help*—Veterans eligible for financial benefits are a special case, and they are particularly upset about the lack of communication between the University and the local Veteran's Administration office. Our problems are a result of the complexity of V.A. regulations and the lack of attention these regulations are receiving on campus. The clerical staff is conscientious, but they do not feel they have sufficient clout to deal with the V.A. There is a lot of student unhappiness on this issue.

25. *International Students Satisfied Now*—I am relieved to report that the international students are among our most satisfied students. Emeritus Professor Mertz has donated his time entirely to integrating international students into campus life and assisting them in the adjustment to our campus. This indeed is a time-consuming requirement. Professor Mertz has become a kind of expert on immigration. Our present arrangement of faculty sponsors has some bright spots, but there are not enough faculty interested in serving as sponsors. One effort to involve people from the community was tremendously successful. You may remember the feature story about it. But the fear I have is, when Dr. Mertz is not available, then what? No one else on the faculty appears to have that kind of interest or time.

26. *Handicapped Students, Visible and Otherwise*—No doubt you have seen the difficulty our wheelchair students are having. While the accounts in the BSU *Daily* were unduly harsh, I would have to say that they were appallingly accurate. We believe that there also are students with less visible handicaps who need assistance. Anecdotes by committee members suggest this, but to be perfectly frank, we are not yet aware of the extent of this problem, let alone whether we can do anything about it. There is a prevailing view that University attitudes on this issue seem callous, and this is an impression we need to dispel.

27. *Our Older Student Population*—Older students are coming to the campus in greater numbers. We have more than 500 people enrolled in our "senior citizen student" program alone, involving

those who are 65 or older. Some of these students have transportation problems, others seem to be very intimidated by our registration process, along with the related bureaucratic procedures to which they must submit. We feel this is holding down enrollments somewhat. It is apparent that in spite of these problems, their contacts on the campus mean as much to this group as the courses they are taking. We have made a very good beginning here, but someone needs to be concerned about the variety of special needs these students present to us.

**28.** *Facilities and Services After Hours*—We note that 15 per cent of our student body is enrolled exclusively in the evening, with another 75 per cent combining day/evening programs. In spite of this, administrative offices, cafeteria, bookstore, etc., are closed at night. Additionally, we have discovered that faculty are unable to find much time to spend with students after evening classes are over. Some remedy in this area, without great expense, should be introduced. The committee agreed that any out-of-class enrichment program for evening students should be a lower priority, at least until basic service needs as noted above are met.

**29.** *Student Health Services Reexamined*—The student health program has failed to meet our expectations. The two hospitals closest to campus, where most of our students are treated, are asking for a surcharge from our Faculty Fee Committee. If this is not illegal, it is indefensible on moral grounds. We have learned that students are simply not going to use the hospitals, preferring to use private physicians of their choice. Unfortunately, other students are just ignoring minor health problems, believing that the hassle with the hospital is more of a discomfort than their illness. We had quite a discussion about contagious diseases in this respect. I think I told you about the student with the measles who would not go home because of the distance; the health people quarantined the room, but that hall has had over thirty cases of the measles. The measles cases may be minor by themselves, but they illustrate a much more serious problem. We must reject out of hand the tired argument from the hospitals about being understaffed to handle our large student caseload. We're paying for this service, a substantial sum I might add, and we need better treatment from the hospitals, from the top of their hierarchy down. A couple of committee members have hinted that we would do well to hire our own staff for the unique health needs of students.

30. *Space Assignment A Problem*—On the preventive side, I can report that Planned Parenthood will come on the campus for a series of programs. Our present complaint is that Ritter, who is doing space assignments this year, gives the activity a very low priority. The committee finds this very annoying; the prevailing view on the committee is that since Ritter is coming up for tenure he just doesn't want to have to deal with extra-class space assignments. It may well be that it is time to assign this activity to someone on a full-time basis. When errors occur in space assignments, tempers generally flare and we've had too much of that in the past two years.

31. *Emotional Health Needs*—The county mental health people report a growing need for staff additions as we negotiate their new contract. They would also like to house one or more people on campus permanently, if space can be found, with a priority concern for the occasional but serious emergencies that occur every year. I can tell you that we are becoming increasingly concerned as we see a growing tendency on their part to favor long-term counseling (I call it therapy) rather than short-term student contacts. We have visited with them about this, but they take the view that this is not a matter anyone can control in advance. I remain skeptical; once one sees the seriousness of a case it should be possible to make the necessary referral. This will permit us to have more students seen for shorter periods, keeping us out of the "therapeutic" business, which we simply cannot afford. Students requiring this kind of assistance should probably leave school until their problems have been successfully resolved. There are several other problems related to mental health which we will pursue as a committee. Though some have stated the opinion that this entire area is not a proper university function, one serious campus incident would likely affect this point of view. Yet we cannot bear heavy expense as a school in this area.

In connection with the above, we can report one innovation which holds some promise. This involves group counseling, encompasses a variety of personal issues. While there are severe space problems involved, if managed properly we will be able to assist larger numbers of students with a marked per-unit reduction in cost. We will watch this development, as it might be applicable in other areas.

**32.** *Voluntary Career Planning Services*—Career planning is handled reasonably well—if we don't "burn out" the faithful few faculty who participate. I do have concern about the fact that many faculty see themselves as teachers, not career specialists, and some faculty argue that if students do not have career objectives they shouldn't be here in the first place. I wish I could report that such a view is unusual, but regrettably it is not.

**33.** *Graduate Placement Services Confused*—In the case of graduating seniors, local and state employers are confused with our arrangements for interviewing. Also, students are not entirely happy with Placement Services, Inc., the firm we selected this year. They are instituting a "locator" fee for all hires, and a fee for all scheduled interviews. They are collecting from both the employer and the student. Certainly we cannot live with that another year. We could do a better job than that ourselves. Have we considered hiring our own staff for this?

We are getting feedback from employers that our students do not always present themselves in the best possible manner. An acquaintance of mine, quite friendly to the University, says that our students need special assistance in both resume writing and interviewing techniques. I believe the College of Business will be able to rectify this matter, and perhaps the Business faculty could establish a program for students from each college who are seeking business careers. Naturally each college will have its own preferred approach, but we have not developed a service through Placement Services, Inc., that addresses these issues.

**34.** *Student Volunteer Opportunities Not Coordinated*—One campus shortcoming we have uncovered will probably be as surprising to you as it was to the committee. This involves our need to coordinate the requests we receive almost daily for volunteer services. There seems to be a great need for assistance in the community; people assume that University students have the time and interest for volunteer work. Many students are interested, but our communication linkages are not effective. Every office seems to go its own way, and the BSU *Daily* has an uneven record in getting the word to students. Maybe we can get a community volunteer to coordinate this effort.

35. *Fraternities Need Direction*—I suppose that no report of this kind would be complete without a reference to fraternities. They appear to be particularly directionless this year and have established a new low as neighbors. Our system of alumni advisors is not working, partly because they are unavailable when needed, and in some cases because of the quality of the individuals. I must say in all candor that some advisors seem less mature than the fraternity men they are supposed to be advising. The sorority system is virtually the same but works much better. The faculty resolution of three years ago, designating faculty to spend time in the houses and assist officers, has never materialized. We really can't expect faculty to be house managers.

36. *Faculty Monitors in Residence Halls*—Our own residence hall system has problems in this respect. Faculty are refusing to live in the halls. Those who do cite long days with sleep interrupted, etc., with their day-time teaching being adversely affected. Students, on the other hand, say that faculty are never available. Conflicts in the hall between faculty and students have, on at least two occasions we are aware of, spilled over into the classroom. Faculty who are serving in the halls want permission to keep alcoholic beverages and would like to have more freedom to entertain, but every faculty request is being met by an equivalent request from students. We have not yet examined this issue thoroughly, but it promises to be complicated from all we can tell to date. Students in the halls are hoping for improvement in the general quality of life there. They say the halls are noisy and messy. They seem to want more control and more freedom, simultaneously. Or I suppose it is fair to say that they want to select their controls and to select their freedoms. The faculty appetite for residential living is rapidly disappearing all over the country, as we understand it.

37. *Off Campus Housing "Rip-Off"*—The off-campus housing situation also illustrates our need for continuing attention to campus

issues. Unfair and unsanitary housing practices are common and I have come to understand what students mean by "rip-off" as they are being gouged unmercifully. Large deposits seem to evaporate, 12-month leases are almost the rule, and attitudes among landlords are infuriating. Three of them met with the committee, and it was the worst meeting we've had all year. If they were on the high seas, they would be guilty of piracy and probably fit candidates for the yardarm.

38. *Legal Problems Increasing*—The landlord problem opened up the area of legal issues. We find that students are facing the garden-variety legal problems of every citizen, due to the lowered age of majority and the tendency toward litigation in the larger society. We discovered that the Law faculty are doing an excellent job in supervising some of their third-year students who provide some services for students—a good example of education and service meshing.

39. *Discipline Policy and Practice Confused*—An interesting by-product of today's legal interests shows up as a spillover from the discipline issues on the campus. Students are bringing their lawyers to hearings, and any hope of educational experiences resulting from discipline is rapidly disappearing. Faculty who are interested in preserving the discipline functions will have to find alternatives to the present approach. We must insist that students accept responsibility for their behavior, but the means of insuring this are becoming increasingly unenforceable. We have more student gamesmanship in this area than in any other. I cannot get into the complex question further in this memo.

40. *Ombudsman's Office Useful*—The ombudsman's office has been successful in dealing with a number of student complaints. Lacy is doing a fine job in this part-time job, but he is overloaded. Our success in this area may mean additional staffing. Students seem very eager to talk if they feel they might get relief from the issues they are presenting. It will be necessary for us to review issues that repeatedly crop up, as they may well point to policy deficiencies that need to be revamped.

41. *Grade Appeals Plan Needed*—We seem to be continually faced with students who believe they have been graded unfairly in

classes. While grading remains a faculty prerogative, this does nothing to soothe the feelings of individual students who believe they have been victimized. We believe there are few students with legitimate complaints, but the issue has taken on enormous symbolic importance. An impartial way of adjudicating these grievances is very badly needed.

42. *Student Workers Union Politicized To What End?*—Need I say that our problems with the Student-Workers Union are serious? The SWU has registered some demonstrable successes, but its lack of understanding of the fragility of higher education is indeed saddening. I think they view their campus politics as both appropriate and fun, but the results have not served us well. A handful of faculty have been influential with the SWU, resulting in some politicization that could have been avoided. Most of these faculty have hidden agendas, but students either don't know it or don't mind. I think it is very wrong to use students in this way, and I know the committee shares this view. The SWU speaks for students, but they have been elected by about 10 per cent of the available electorate. Although I know this isn't their fault, I wish they would show some evidence of recognizing it. No one works with these students in a sustained way. Someone is needed who might have as a primary motive the growth and development of the students. I know most of the SWU leaders, and they are trying to be responsive, but they are simply pulled in too many directions. As they look back on their leadership experiences, I don't think these students will feel that they were served very well. Except for the activist-oriented faculty, the professoriate shows no interest in this area at all, unless they are touched by a specific issue. This is a crucial need, as it affects the environment of the campus, and we will give it the attention it deserves. We may suggest that the University give someone the assignment of helping these students work in more positive ways.

43. *Research Needs Not Served*—There appears to be a general understanding that the campus is a unique and complex environment, but beyond this recognition we are doing very little about it. While the value of research is uniformly applauded by our colleagues, we have not used the tools of research to mend the problems we know exist. There are pockets of interest among the

faculty, and perhaps that interest can be nurtured. But first comes research to know what to do. We have no practical means for either research or for nurture, once interests and trends are identified.

**44.** *A Home For Student Cares?*—There is a lack of collaborative, sustained effort to make this campus a warm, humane place, a place comprising people who care for students in a personal sense. Academic excellence is still king, a position I can acknowledge as appropriate, but not to the exclusion of all else. Fortunately we have faculty who do care, or things would be worse than they are now. What we don't have is sufficient faculty time, and a program to bring some coherence to individual efforts. We will continue to seek ways to integrate the issues, problems, feelings, and human ingredients which students bring to the campus, with the demanding formal curriculum they are asked to manage. This is not going to be easy.

I hope you will pardon the length of this memorandum, but you asked me to try to reflect on those issues to which we have at least paid some attention. While I feel exhausted as I send the memorandum, I have not exhausted all of the issues I intended to raise.

It must suffice for the moment to say that we are looking at the special problems outlined by commuting students; the failure we see in developing student organizations on the campus, and the need to provide those organizations with some faculty leadership; the system of grading; measuring student development; the concerns of students who have pursued an education for several years and more who need to be counseled as they stop-in and stop-out; ways in which we can individualize instruction without sacrificing standards; using student work experiences to better advantage; the participation of students in governance; the role of intramurals on the campus and the role of sports as lifetime leisurely pursuits; the allocation and use of student fees; as well as other issues which are bound to develop as we pursue our assignment. You can see that the task you set for us is formidable indeed.

I am optimistic about our ability to make some useful recommendations to you, but, clearly, some will cost significant dollars. The inescapable reality is that we can cut faculty time only so many ways, and it is thin now. It seems to me that we may well have to look toward a group of faculty who might find the kinds of issues and problems raised here to be sufficiently challenging and worthwhile to pursue on a full-time career basis.

Office of the President
De Loema Center

Dr. Agnes Webb
Professor, English Literature
Beta State University

Dear Dr. Webb:

Your comments are almost overwhelming. If this is a progress report, I am afraid to think what the final report will be like. We have been a very attractive institution in days past; our faculty are excellent, and our curriculum is sound. Yet, if we are going to retain our students and meet changing conditions, as you have pointed out, we will need to consider major improvements for the life of students.

We will take your final report seriously, I assure you. I am not sure we can afford all that you may recommend. Yet to take these matters lightly could result in far higher costs than the cost of instituting your ultimate recommendations.

I am intrigued by your idea of seeing if a group of faculty might be willing to pursue these challenges on a full-time career basis. At least, we will need some persons to coordinate our efforts.

We'll talk soon.

Sincerely,

J.M. Marshall
President

JMM:sp

# The Odyssey (or, How Did I Miss the Sirens?)

IT ALL BEGAN at Airlie House in Virginia, in the fall of 1975, when several leaders of NIRAD met to organize the next thrust of its research and development program. The head nodders came out ahead of the head shakers by a half-nod, and a book idea developed enough momentum to warrant another session in Denver in December. In the group in Denver were Jim Appleton, Earle Clifford, John Blackburn, Jim Rhatigan, Rich Harpel, and myself, Channing Briggs. The definitive idea of the book—to portray styles, values, and beliefs of effective administrators—was born there. The taping of our brainstorming session (with a few short recesses for deleted expletives and accompanying catharses) was the beginning of recordings that eventually provided enough tape to go around the world—of our ideas—at least twice.

Jim Appleton and Chan attempted to reduce the discussion to prime concerns in nine categories. These were shared with the NIRAD Board, who were also asked to certify the book as its first priority. When the Board met in Dallas in April 1976, further refinements were made. By mid-May, Tom Dutton and Jim Appleton became the first respondents to the questionnaire containing some 83 questions, posed in their first, pristine—and primitive—form, because the sequencing and wording were still to be finalized. But the ice was broken, the project was underway.

It was to become a latter-day Odyssey. Eight authors, eight interviews, eight visits with long-time friends; from May until late July; coast to coast, into the nation's breadbasket, to the foot of the Rockies, a jaunt of some 13,000 miles. How Circe or the Sirens were missed must have been a studio oversight.

For the twentieth century Ulysses, Tennyson's great lines brought pertinence, challenge, and a rousing sendoff:

> Come my friends
> 'Tis not too late to seek a newer world.
> Push off, and setting well in order smite

The sounding furrows; for my purpose holds
To sail beyond the sunset, and the baths
Of all the western stars, until I die.
It may be that the gulfs will wash us down.
It may well be we shall touch the Happy Isles,
And see the great Achilles, whom we knew.
Tho' much is taken, much abides: and tho'
We are not now that great strength which in old days
Moved earth and heaven; that which we are, we are;
One equal temper of heroic hearts,
Made weak by time and fate, but strong in will
To strive, to seek, to find and not to yield.

That first Ulysses sailed the Mediterranean for decades. The 1976 Ulysses, with somewhat faster passage and a more exacting itinerary, made his voyage in a matter of months to meet a deadline that never burdened Ulysses I: a publishing date!

In America's Bicentennial year, the 1976 Odyssey was a festival of historical and contemporary rewards: Coming into Philadelphia we flew within 500 feet of the Queen's yacht, the *Britannia*. Earlier that day we had thrilled at the tall ships in the Hudson, as much of America had participated in person or on television in a memorable and splendid celebration of its 200th birthday in New York City.

A month earlier our latter-day Ulysses had seen the blooming of the nation's bread-basket—miles and miles of "amber waves of grain" in the great state of Kansas. In late July the spectacle was the Rockies, majestic though stripped of their white mantle by the warm, Colorado sun. As he got caught up by the bicentennial spirit, Ulysses II was tempted to emulate

**If we are serious about style and personality showing, then Channing will not let us get by without letting him write something about how it looks to him. It ought to capture the spirit of the thing and encourage one to read the book.**

Kate Smith in her tuneful blessing of America. Fortunately, this Ulysses demurred, and to this day the tender eardrums of friends can thank his restraint against that frightening impulse.

The contributors, from Union's ivied walls to the Trojan stronghold at USC, were eight unusual persons who had attained the presidency of NASPA. Everyone was willing to share basic beliefs and deep commitments to the fundamental human concerns and efforts attending the wondrous emergence of tomorrow's generation—a challenging, rewarding role in each institution. Some personal observations about each participant:

Pacing the floor as he spoke, punctuating his crisp commentary with emphatic declarations, Earle Clifford responded briskly as he, Jack Boland and I worked through the interview in his home. The interviewers had arrived from Frostburg too late to savor his office niche at Fairleigh Dickinson University. His wife had just brought Earle's Fred Turner Distinguished Service citation from the photographer, framed and ready for hanging. This accolade has since joined many others on one wall of the Clifford Manse.

Earle was never verbose, nor had he assembled notes anywhere but in his mind. At times he would take a couple minutes to shape his reasoning and rationale before delivering his thoughts in a barrage as cogent as it was rapid. So, as on so many other occasions I had watched him in action—awaiting phone calls from a national newspaper or interrupting a prolonged harangue in a meeting with clarifying observations, solid arguments, here he was, much as I'd observed him through the last decade: no hesitancy, no mugwump maybes, no tentative whispers, just solid stuff, efficiently packaged and clearly stated.

It was a pleasure except for one arresting moment. Earle's son is a developing gymnast. Across one door frame was an exercise bar. Earle and Jack could duck under it with ease. For me, it was nearly a deep knee bend! I'd parked my bags in one of his upstairs rooms. Came time to leave. Bags secured, venerable Ulysses here goes piling out, forgetting the gymnastic hurdle. Precisely! The immovable object won again, taking Ulysses 1976 to his knees. None of the celestial bodies seen even resembled a Siren. Two weeks later I queried Earle about removing the "feller" of travelers. No, it had not been removed, nor had the bloodstains been removed from the rug!

Prior to visiting Earle I had sojourned in the Allegheny Mountains on a visit with Alice Manicur. How does one fly to Frostburg, Maryland?!? One may begin at Washington or Baltimore on the East with a pilot who is seemingly a surgically implanted component of a thin-skinned, twin-engine bird which responds instantly and frighteningly to every type of force and fury in the aerodynamic dictionary. One might even name the mini-clipper "Turbulent Tina." Storm clouds were not to be flown over, but to be circumnavigated. Turbulent Tina threaded through many of them at 6,000 feet; it is a humbling feeling to see a storm cloud belching 10,000 feet above! Jet travel has denied this era of so many voyageur thrills! In this mini-clipper the thunderheads were awesome monsters, dwarfing the upstart mechanical intruder. The passengers spent great gobs of empathy in mutual concern for survival. All this was augmented by the vocal concern of a canine passenger who was sure he was whining away his last breaths of life. Whether it was the scared pup or our shared concerns, it helped support that tiny envelope of people through the perils of the illimitable air.

One flies into Cumberland, Maryland, to get to Frostburg. The Allegheny range looks like the beautiful rolling carpet of a deciduous forest. The airport sits on a small plateau. A too-low approach will meet a formidable wall that will cancel that pilot's error forever. But the men at the controls were a confident lot; at least, they missed the wall. John Lowe and Alice met me, gave me the tour highlights on the way to the campus. Within 10 minutes in Alice's office as preparations for the interview were made, e.g., checking the audio, getting the tapes lined up, her president ushered in a former board member and successful banker in another city. What a wonderful hello to Alice! How he had missed her in the intervening years. That welcome typified the visit—warm, hospitable, candid, and forthright.

We worked into the night, interrupted only  by an enjoyable dinner with the Lowes. Quite aware of this traveler's disdain for four-footed felines, they admonished and isolated their favorite pet. Next morning I met with all the staff for a rousing exchange of quips, quotes, and questions before taking the Cumberland airborne Toonerville Trolley to get to Newark by way of Washington.

Prior to the trip east I had already conducted interviews with Tom Dutton and Jim Appleton in late May and Chet Peters and Jim Rhatigan in early June. Tom had a meeting in Los Angeles in mid-May so he met with us after Jim and I had worked half a day putting the finishing touches on the interview questions. They were the guinea pigs, as it were. Would the questions spark adequate responses? What topics were overlooked? What questions might be less provocative, possibly deleted? Over the long afternoon the three of us pressed ahead. There were many recollections of Oakland University in Michigan, where Tom and Jim had enjoyed several years together. Banter about the public-private university competition relieved the monotony of repetitive passages. The probing and pressing of the afternoon was an acid test of the product of months of extended communication following the Denver Decision of December.

During that afternoon in Los Angeles, I saw these two able men, Tom and Jim, in typical, productive exchange: Amazingly compatible, strikingly collaborative, and stimulated by mutual respect. They have known each other for years and can almost predict the responses of the other. Jim would say: "Tom would respond this way, but from my viewpoint I would modify his response to this observation." And Tom might offer a similar rejoinder, even to the point of offering Jim's rationale for the varying viewpoint! This was an exhilarating session!

It was easy to slip back in time. On one of my trips to Detroit, Tom had arranged for a staff dinner at Oakland so that I could see his crowd in action—Fred Smith, Jim Appleton, Ed Birch, Pat Houtz, Manuel Pierson, Doug Woodard. These good friends are now first-line deans or vice-presidents. Tom has always been able to attract highly competent staff.

During his NASPA presidency one never had to guess where Tom stood. And his organizational style was something to behold. I could just predict, almost to the hour, his telephone call prior to an Executive Committee meeting. His accountability and responsibility were always assured: no question, no vacillation.

To see Jim interact with Tom is a joy. These two may be closer than brothers for they share great respect for one another. Yet they are unlike in many attributes. Tom's deliberations contrast with Jim's initiated options. Jim's energetic dash differs from Tom's amazingly, unruffled administrative order. Tom's uncanny ability to ask the critical, probing question is yet another mark of his sagacity. Jim may move his programs more by the sheer power of his imaginative initiation.

Tom never allows for Locke's "tabula rasa" approach to a discussion about a problem. He will lay his own model or option or assumption on the line, against which other ideas may be measured. Jim may structure discussion modes to get specific results, yet he tends to have great faith in the potential dividends from the group process, directed quietly by his strong convictions.

The project was actually getting launched, I was assured. Jim would interrupt now and then to monitor the process: "How are we doing? Are we getting what we hoped? How's it going?" The day ended with tapes full of good information; if all eight offer as specific a set of answers revealing their true beliefs, I concluded, we had the makings of an interesting book.

Four weeks later, I left Kansas City at 7:30 a.m. to meet an old friend, senior athlete, and wood-carver par excellence, Chet Peters, at Kansas State. Kansas is flat but it does cover a lot of ground. Corn was waist-high in a few places but high water had helped burn out acres of it in low-lying draws. Chet had a room reserved in a local hostelry. We had a quick lunch, then walked a few blocks to his office.

The Kansas State Ad Building is an old one. Through its corridors have passed thousands and thousands of students. The building almost reminded me of my first visit to Eton just before the war. Laid about 1440, Eton's stone floors now have noticeable depressions which the young men of Eton have worn during its 500(!) years. Kansas State is not that hoary, but one senses a venerable history.

How could one miss Chet's office, filled with great carvings, including the one he used at the Denver conference. The woods are rich, the treatment richer, and there was the sculptor himself. Audiovisual equipment ready to go, but first look at his office. It is not grand, nor heavy with perquisites like thick carpeting, two acres of desk top, or two Picassos on the wall. But one feels at home in Chet's office. And the occupant is a tradition at KSU, having been there in various capacities for more than 30 years.

He had cleared his calendar so that he could proceed with the interview uninterrupted. It was good to hear his solid, decisive tones again; they were as sure and sonorous as when he left the Executive Committee in 1973. I shall always remember that heartfelt "so long" at the Ben Franklin in 1973. Earlier, he and I had walked miles, finding a great eating place, deep within the less palatable neighborhood, far south of Independence Square. Somehow, our vulnerability seemed less because Chet was my companion—a man without an ounce of rancor or rage in his being.

Themes began to take shape from his responses: a long history at KSU; student participation in decision processes as standard operating procedures; friendly but firm confrontation on issues that mattered; and respect for all with whom he worked.

The afternoon rambled by. Soon we were enjoying a steak dinner in his home with his wife and son, who had been taking classes at KSU for the past year. Chet had received a lot of unlaundered, unfiltered feedback from him: valuable correctives to a vice-president's perceptions. Like his office, Chet's home is modest and hospitable. Kansas sun prompted him to charcoal the steaks outside. Table conversation at the meal was full of recollections and comments about the recent trip to Japan. For years, Chet had competed in the senior nationals. The previous year he had added the steeplechase to his half-mile and mile events. His rugged frame fit the same size clothes it did ten years ago. No week goes by without running the requisite miles.

After dinner and goodbyes to the family, we toured the huge campus more than half-filled with "Aggie" accoutrements. Cattle, sheep, poultry, hogs took up a fair piece of all that Kansas real estate. The wafting breezes assured me that agriculture has a built-in organic component! We saw a few practicum students caring properly for their charges.

After another two hours of interviewing, I took early leave, for tomorrow it was another good morning's trip to Wichita for an interview with the Mark Twain of the Plains, genial Jim Rhatigan.

The next day was June 10th, another warm Kansas day. I was on the road by 8:45, headed for Wichita from Manhattan. By noon I had checked into the motel; presently I was in sight of the stadium erected to demonstrate the power and glory of the "Shockers." Hardly the symbol of erudition, thought I. In another five minutes I was given the royal treatment by Joan Gleeson, Jim's right arm.

Wichita State University's campus is extensive, yet it is an urban campus. The young institution has the appearance of affluency and enjoys an *au courant* flair: fine art museum, beautiful outdoor statuary, wise landscaping, and a number of buildings whose pedigree is certified by outstanding architects. The statuary is not flaunted but rather seems to blend into the total campus plan. So, though recently developed, the setting augured well for an interview with an enthusiastic, well-organized, and stimulating Jim Rhatigan.

Jim's office is a combination of library, hospitable meeting place, and efficient work station. It was easy to see that Jim often accomplished as much by roaming the campus as he did staying in his office. His pipe between thumb and index finger while he speaks, Jim is a tumble of quips and comments as he takes stock of his charges firsthand, not by way of some reporting process.

At lunch we saw Paul Magelli, one of Jim's academic colleagues serving as Dean of the Liberal Arts and Sciences College. Paul had known Fred Turner very well at Urbana. We talked about Fred's great library, his decades of service to the Association, contributions of considerable magnitude. The campus interview went by quickly. After dinner at Jim's Faculty Club, we visited his wife and daughter at his home, where he keeps an office just as orderly as his institutional niche.

We spent another three hours on the interview. Jim is not equivocal. His sense of humor is infectious—and not without intellectual depth. I was reminded of his contributions at San Francisco: On Sunday evening he was the savant, drawing from the works of Nevitt Sanford and Ted Newcomb in his presentation. On Tuesday, he was the master chairman, running the business meeting with gusto, kidding Jim Appleton on his past president status, which he himself would inherit the next day.

One month after visiting with Jim Rhatigan I was met at the Albany Airport by Mark and Nancy Smith. Mark was now at Union, after having spent much of his career at Denison. Mark and Nancy were in campus housing. Their lot was to inherit a former fraternity house, in consideration for Mark's long interest in the fraternal life. The ceilings are at least 12 feet high. The rooms are large and the walls offer a challenge and an opportunity to creative people like the Smiths. Mark is a sculptor and wood-collage creator. Nancy's sewing skills would shame a dressmaker. The results of their efforts in this cavernous refuge from campus cares were phenomenal. Mark's wood sculptures range from the head of an Indian to some bizarre tricks of nature. One bird's head, as diminutive as a hummingbird's, sat on the body of a pterodactyl. Nancy's contribution, a flamboyance of multicolored banners, reminded me of the courtyard horse-racing pennants that flutter everywhere at the annual Siena event. Not one of them showed Greek letters!

The wall decor was merely the setting. In one room was a huge refrigerator, well-stocked with beer and soft drinks. On an adjacent wall was a large dartboard. It was easy to see that the Smith residence is a campus gathering spot, as it proved while I was there, but minor by comparison to usual days. Dozens of students and faculty make their way to this friendly home day in and day out.

I had not seen Mark in four years. His interest in the north woods continues, particularly in his blanched driftwood collection. A towering 6 feet, 8 inches, he can reach any low-hanging bulb on campus—by hand or head, which may help account for his thinning hair.

Mark was ready for the interview with reams of notes. The transcript of our interview covered more than 70 pages. His exceptional investment of time in a constant effort to know all students on campus was happening at Union. When I queried Mark on this tack, he replied that his memory was so bad that he had to resort to extreme mnemonic devices. My gentle, thoughtful response: "Bosh!"

Most of his declarations came forth reinforced by solid rationale, but there were humble and tentative explorations as well. The all-time maverick, conversation manipulator, and exploder of myths had mellowed. As cook and host, he approached perfection. Of course, Nancy was the key! She was wrapping up a master's in social organization while working full time as a computer expert, but the kitchen functioned as though she had never left it.

It had been a great reunion with a delightful couple in the biggest house I have ever slept in! Mark's words would keep our transcriber busy for days.

Only John Blackburn's interview remained. It was scheduled for July 30 in the Hilton Inn in Denver, where so many NASPA Executive Committee meetings had been held in the late 60s and early 70s. John was already getting his gravelly voice lubricated with coffee when I arrived. We also hoped for a meeting with the two Jims and Alice before leaving for Vail to attend the ACE-NASPA Institute that weekend. John was also well prepared with notes. By noon we were halfway through the effort. I pleaded for a short swim before lunch. We resumed at 1:30.

John's answers, as always, were punctuated with regular petitions to the deities. Such rhetorical emphases were usually reinforced by a sweep of his left arm, always from left to right. He was a kind of Harry Truman, who emphasized his points with a staccato left at the 1956 Democratic Convention in Chicago. Nor were these emphases some last-minute remiscences or revelations; for John challenges Jim Rhatigan as our best-read, best-informed past president.

John's home revealed more of Chet Peters' sculpture. Impressed by Chet's presentation at the Denver Conference, John commissioned him to create a Madonna in heavy wood as a gift to his wife. That piece, revealing humility, piety, and beauty, stands in the entryway of John's home.

John emphasized the overall goals and objectives of the institution as the guiding criteria for all actions of the University. He praised Chancellor

Mitchell as a capable and prophetic voice in higher education, one who would continuously refine the direction of the University upon just and valid grounds. He also emphasized the need to develop flair and excitement in his staff, in student leadership. He spoke of community and the need to develop trust and consideration among people. A listener cannot be long in John's company without sensing a tremendous flow of energy for new ideas, for a better tomorrow. One line will stay with me a long time. He said he looked forward to the day a student would sue the university (any university) for *not* inculcating a set of ethical values in the student. This wry approach was reinforced at a later meeting in Washington, when Jim Appleton noted that John had a "killer instinct," once an appropriate opening occurred. He and Earle have for years been creative synthesizers, bringing resolution to unanswered issues. And few of their actions and ideas stand on anything but basic ethical considerations.

The first round was over. Integrating the efforts of the eight might prove difficult, but we were on our way. Nearly 500 pages of transcribed notes had been generated. Many cogent ideas and countless nuances needed to be assessed and assimilated. Throughout the effort rang one overriding phrase: The road of leadership is traversed in many vehicles; the best of the lot is sheer integrity and competence. That may be the finest gold to be mined from *Pieces of Eight*.